Images of Tudor Kingship

Images of Tudor Kingship

Sydney Anglo

© Sydney Anglo 1992
First published 1992

Typeset by Setrite Typesetters
Printed by Biddles Ltd., Guildford
Surrey, Great Britain
for the publishers
B A Seaby Ltd
7 Davies Street
London W1Y 1LL

ISBN 185264 034 0

British Library Cataloguing in Publication Data

CONTENTS

LIST OF FIGURES

ACKNOWLEDGEMENTS

The author and publishers are grateful to the following who have supplied illustrations and have given permission for their reproduction.

Times Newspapers Limited, (1); Society of Antiquaries, (2,5,15,16,17,18,24); The British Library, (6,8,9,11,12,19,20,21,30,31); College of Arms, (4); by kind permission of the Provost and Scholars of King's College, Cambridge, (7); Royal Armouries, (22); Bodleian Library, (23); The Royal Mint, (26).

INTRODUCTION

On 27 April 1989, at Coquelles near Calais — to the sound of applause, fireworks, the French and British national anthems, and miscellaneous folk dances — Henry VIII King of England and Francis I King of France had their third personal meeting after an interval of 457 years. On this occasion, it is true, the mighty monarchs did not walk, talk, or even move. They merely stood, 6-metres-high polystyrene statues, one on either side of the Eurotunnel breakthrough, as the 350 tonne Japanese boring machine, *Virginie*, completed the shaft at the Coquelles terminal.

The choice of Henry and Francis to symbolize Anglo-French co-operation was not, from an historical point of view, entirely happy. The two kings heartily disliked each other and neither of their two previous encounters, at the Field of Cloth of Gold in 1520 and at Boulogne in 1532, had been politically productive. Their belated reappearance at Coquelles in 1989 does, however, raise some interesting questions concerning images, their persistence, effect and interpretation. Few of the audience on that occasion, and few of those who enjoyed the photograph published next morning in *The Times*, would have had any difficulty either in identifying the two kings or grasping that they represented England and France (see Fig. 1). But what would a sixteenth-century audience have made of it all? Few, apart from court-iers, would ever have seen the monarchs; fewer still would have had a glimpse of the portraits by Holbein and Clouet; and hardly anybody at all would even have heard of either artist.

One of the greatest obstacles barring the way to a sensible appreciation of the ways in which Renaissance rulers were perceived by their contemporaries is that we know a great deal more about these kings and queens than did even the best informed of their subjects. It is true that we cannot hear their voices, interview them or see them in the flesh: but in these respects we are no worse off than all but their tiny circle of intimates. We know something of their physical appearance from the portraits which we may see in galleries and exhibitions, or

Fig. 1. 'French Tunnel reaches ... Calais', photograph by Tim Bishop published in *The Times*, 28 April 1989.

reproduced in books which are constantly at hand. We can travel about the countryside viewing paintings, tapestries, *objets d'art*, and architectural remains; or we may scrutinize detailed photographs of these in lavishly illustrated volumes at home or in a library. We study and compare the writings of Tudor authors in handy scholarly editions, all conveniently glossed, annotated and indexed. We read royal correspondence and state papers with a privileged ease and comprehensiveness denied to any contemporary. And should some literary or iconographic riddle confront us, then we may soon solve it by recourse to shelves full of monographs, articles and works of reference.

To point out that contemporaries did not share these advantages is to state the obvious. Yet it is precisely the obvious which is most frequently overlooked when, as in recent years, scholars have become increasingly interested in the role played by myths and images in public affairs and have liberally deployed the languages of rhetoric, semiotics and social anthropology in their attempts to explain the nature of Renaissance political symbolism. The desire to explicate symbols and to rationalize their evocative power is wholly understandable for there is a magnetic attraction in attempting to resolve mysteries and to unlock the past with a magical master key. Nor can it be denied that these varied approaches have yielded rich results, elucidating the convolutions of Renaissance erudition and making us aware of the diverse intellectual traditions which may sometimes lie behind a familiar emblem.

But there has been a price to pay. Many attempts to expound the political implications of paintings, love poetry, occasional verse, court festivals and a wide variety of other source materials, are characterized by a deadly seriousness. The element of play is almost entirely ignored, and it is sometimes impossible — in the midst of these earnest analyses — to imagine that princes and courtiers may have organized and participated in tournaments, masques and dances for recreation; written, read and recited poems for enjoyment; watched plays and sung songs for delight; or adorned their dwellings and their persons for pleasure.

The language and tone of many discussions of royal imagery are too elevated and tendentious. They *assume* the very things that ought to be *proved*: governmental planning in the creation and propagation of political symbolism on the one hand; and the existence of a sophisticated and informed public response on the other. It has thus become commonplace to write about the 'projection' of the image of royalty as though Renaissance potentates employed advertising agencies and public re-lations teams; about 'propaganda' as though these monarchs were each served by their own equivalent of Joseph Goebbels; and about 'princely patronage' as if early modern states had arts councils and cultural policies. Conversely, emblems and devices are discussed as though the average sixteenth-century citizen were a walking compendium of Neoplatonic theory — with the whole of some iconographic encyclo-paedia, such as Valeriano Bolzani's *Hieroglyphica*, committed to memory and ready for instant recall — wandering abroad in a world where seemingly innocent references by word or image to animals, vegetables and minerals were, in fact, cryptic allusions to profound doctrines; where royal portraits were regarded as 'votive images'; and where scraps of eulogistic doggerel by aspiring authors were expressions of a 'cult' of monarchy. Yet it is difficult to demonstrate that arcane utterance was the normal mode of literary and artistic discourse; that such portraits were really being offered up to a deity as propitiation; or that such verses were the fruits of a genuinely religious devotion to the monarch rather than of patriotic fervour or, at worst, a venal desire for material advancement.

The hushed and reverential tone favoured by students of iconology is especially inapposite for England in the fifteenth and sixteenth centuries. It is true that the Tudors are the best known and most readily recognized English royal house. Their name conjures up a gallery of familiar characters: the thin, crafty-eyed, avaricious Henry VII; the arrogant persecutor of wives, 'Bluff King Hal'; the priggish, perennial 'Young Josaiah', Edward VI; the ailing, unhappy 'Bloody Mary'; and the tight-lipped oval mask of the triumphant, ever-virgin 'Good Queen Bess'. Even more familiar are their badges: the 'red dragon dreadful', the portcullis, the greyhound, and the 'rose both red

and white'. Indeed, so infallibly and instantaneously do these badges
call to mind the house of Tudor that they may fairly be described as
dynastic hieroglyphs.

The individual style of each monarch — depending as it did upon
personality and perceived needs — differed enormously. Similarly,
there is a marked contrast between our own perception of the early
Tudors and of Elizabeth I resulting, at least in part, from the accelerated
scope and volume of printing in the latter half of the sixteenth century.
Yet the distinctive signs which indicated the Tudor dynasty were all
established at the outset of Henry VII's reign and remained constant
thereafter. Tudor dynastic symbolism was extremely simple, but the
simplicity is by no means self-evident: and it is this seeming paradox
which provides the theme and structure of the present book. As I have
suggested, a good deal of attention has been devoted to how and why
symbolism functions: but none whatever has been paid to its limitations
and failures. I am concerned, therefore, to examine dynastic imagery
not only within its intellectual context but also within its practical
context — the context of what was *possible* in Renaissance England. Did
contemporaries have any general theories governing the function and
manipulation of images? What were the signs which distinguished the
Tudors from other dynasties, and how sophisticated were they? Did
they evolve spontaneously, or were they consciously planned? For
whom were they intended; and how were they deployed? I begin with a
consideration of some of the traditions, both theoretical and practical,
relating to the external manifestation of monarchical power in Tudor
England. This is followed by chapters devoted to each of the three
principal genealogical traditions — the British descent, the Lancastrian
connection, and the union of the houses of York and Lancaster —
which underlay the badges and emblems used by Henry Tudor, his
son, and his three grandchildren. And the final chapter examines the
various practical means available for the display of monarchy, and
considers their very circumscribed efficacy. I do not discount the skill
and learning with which scholars have illuminated some very difficult
areas of Renaissance political symbolism. I merely offer a tiny tincture
of scepticism, and suggest that there may be other ways of regarding
these matters.

Chapter One

IMAGES OF KINGSHIP: DYNASTIC HIEROGLYPHS

Modern scholarship has made us acutely sensitive to the political iconography of Renaissance Europe. We know a great deal about the imagery not only of the great territorial monarchs such as the Holy Roman Emperors, and the Kings of France and Spain, but also of the cluster of petty princelings in Italy where the gap between the pretensions of political imagery and the realities of political power widened into a chasm. The iconographical foundations of early modern kingship have been subjected to intensive academic scrutiny and have been shown to comprise many diverse elements: sacral and cosmic kingship in the ancient world; the rich ideological legacy of both imperial and papal Rome; the ceremonial opulence of Byzantium; and the legalistic and hieratic complexities of medieval Christendom. In addition to these, the relevance of Renaissance theories concerning the power of images has been forcefully argued, together with the ways in which these could be manipulated to give visual expression to earlier political ideas.

The difficulty with all these traditions is that they dealt largely in abstractions, and the images associated with them were generalized. They were about monarchy itself and had virtually nothing to do with any individual prince or dynasty. No ruler could ignore them, and every ruler sought to deploy them. Yet they were personal to none. There was plenty of material ready-made to represent kingship — just as there were plenty of experts who could organize a coronation or royal funeral so that it fulfilled all the symbolic requirements — but it was also necessary for rulers to make themselves, their dynasty and their possessions instantly recognizable. And here we run headlong into very complex questions: on the one hand, of intentionality and serendipity in the creation of dynastic imagery; and, on the other, of public response and comprehension.

The fact of the matter is that, whatever conditions may have prevailed elsewhere in Europe, in England throughout the Tudor era there was never any consistent theory about the function of political images. Consequently, no such theory could be translated into practice. The imagery of Tudor kingship resulted rather from a series of *ad hoc* expedients and the successful exploitation of a number of traditions which had been, or could be, associated with monarchical power.

Magnificence

The utility of princely magnificence — those splendid appearances which served as the external sign of intrinsic power — was as fully appreciated in England as elsewhere. Writers and politicians knew about it from their own experience; from its theoretical enunciation in the fourth book of Aristotle's *Ethics*; and from the reiteration of *that* in countless treatises *De regimine principum*, all explaining the difference between prodigality and liberality, and all insisting that it behoves princes to spend their money not only wisely but also lavishly.[1] The fundamental Aristotelian principle was enshrined in the prolegomena to the Royal Household Ordinance of 1478, which stressed that, while prodigality was to be avoided, it was more important to eschew avarice 'which is the werse extremite, and a vice moore odiouse and detestable' (Myers 1959: 211–28).

Scholars and their princely pupils would also have been familiar with the pseudo-Aristotelian hotch-potch known, in the West, as the *Secretum Secretorum* where Aristotle tells Alexander the Great:

> It sitteth to his dignite honorably to be clothed, and ever in faire garnementis and robes passyng other in fairnesse. And he shold were dere, rich and straunge ornamentes. Fittyng also it is for a kyng to have a prerogatif in his arraie above all others, wherby his dignite is worshiped and made faire, his pouste [power] or myght not hurt, and due reverence to hym at all tyme yeve.
> (Manzalaoui 1977: 36–7)

It was Henry VI's failure to observe this injunction which disenchanted many of his followers when, during his progress in 1470, the inept monarch always seemed to be wearing the same blue velvet gown, as though he had nothing else to change into. The whole affair was regarded contemptuously as more like a play than 'the shewyng of a prynce to wynne mennys hertys' (Thomas and Thornley 1938: 215).

Sir John Fortescue, Chief Justice of the King's Bench in the reign of Henry VI, devoted a chapter of his treatise, *The Governance of England*, to 'The King's Extraordinarie Charges' in which he explained that, in addition to dressing splendidly, a monarch had to furnish his palaces richly, encourage building works, ensure that his ambassadors were sent abroad suitably equipped, and that their counterparts — foreign ambassadors visiting England — were generously received. If a king did not or could not behave in this way then, said Fortescue, he lived not according to his rank, 'but rather in miserie, and in more subgeccion than doth a private person' (Fortescue, ed. Plummer 1885: 123–6). Several generations and two dynasties later, the same lesson was still being repeated to the young King Edward VI by William Forrest who declared, in *The Pleasaunt Poesye of Princelie Practice* (1548: verses 233–6), that no expense on gold, fine cloths, silks and precious stones, was too great for a king to 'glase his glorie in princelieste wise'. Just as a prince must have no equal in his apparel, so 'in cowrte keepinge his plentie must passe'; and his food, drink, plate and glass must be beyond comparison. The king's position is summed up by Forrest in a line of memorable execrability: 'Hys powre, peereles, without peere must appeere' (Manzalaoui 1977: 454–5).

When, early in the 1470s, a committee of the most powerful men in the land compiled for Edward IV a detailed survey of the functioning of the English royal household, *The Black Book of the Household*, they cited a number of precedents. The foremost was no less a monarch than King Solomon, the 'exemplar of householding', who astonished the Queen of Sheba by the abundance of his table, by the order within which his magnificence was manifested and by the splendour and quality of those who served him. The Queen was particularly impressed by his officers, formed 'in astate and degrees, all thing executing after theyr occupacions and chargez to the high excellence of the king'. She was dumbfounded to see that these men, in their demeanour and rich array, might each be likened to a king in her own land; and she marvelled 'more hugely' at

> the stedfast obervaunces of the good rulis, apoyntments, and ordinaunces for the householde, to kepe the ministres thereof from any breche, outrage, reproche, or nicetie, making ordynat reverentz aftyr the distinccions of every high or low degre, and as pepull to straungers cherefull, so many under obedyence in one house'.
>
> (Myers 1959: 81)

After Solomon's ordered magnificence, *The Black Book* discusses a number of English courtly prototypes – Lud, Cassibellanus, Harde-canute, Henry I and, most significant, Edward III whose household 'was the house of very polycye and flowre of Inglond, the furst setter of sertayntez among his domestycall meyne, uppon a grounded rule'. This was the art of court life: fixed routine; specified duties; clear demarcations; a place for everybody and everybody in his place (Anglo 1990: 66–98). The purpose of this organization is to achieve the ideal of princely magnificence which the compilers of *The Black Book* define by summarizing the appropriate section of Aristotle's *Ethics*. The magnificent ruler disburses great sums of money tastefully, like an artist; the results are proportionate to the outlay; the aim is always noble; and the primary concern is with the beauty and quality of the end product, not with any consideration of cheapness and economy. Magnificence is liberality on a grand scale, but it must never degenerate into prodigality. In short, says *The Black Book*, the King 'wull have his goodes dispended but not wasted. Et sic scribitur Ecclesiastes. DOMUS REGIS EDIFICABITUR SAPIENTIA' (Myers 1959: 86–7).

Magnificence was obligatory for effective kingship. So, too, was the ritual display of that magnificence – another aspect of kingship touched upon in the *Secretum Secretorum* which issues a stern warning against rulers mingling too freely with their inferiors, for familiarity 'bringeth contempt'. It would be much better to follow the example of the Indians who have established that their king appears once a year among his people: 'in kyngly apparaill and with host armed, siting nobly upon a courser arraied in his fairest array of armes'. The common people are made to stand a good way off, and 'the states of nobles and barons to be aboute hym' (Manzalaoui 1977: 37). It was some conception of this sort which underlay the progresses of medieval and renaissance princes through their dominions; the display of regal raiment and riches on specific feast days; and the ritual crown-wearings which were made much of by the Yorkist kings who, in the words of C. A. J. Armstrong, thereby intended 'to stabilize, by an appeal to the visual senses, social conditions which had become dangerously fluid' (Armstrong 1983: 92).

The grandest occasion of all, and the one most saturated with symbolic significance, was the coronation: and the practical dimension of this mystic ceremony was especially well enunciated by Sir John Elyot in *The Book named the Governour* (1531). The relevant passage occurs in a chapter devoted to 'Justice distributive' (Elyot, ed. Croft 1883: I, 188–201). The principal part of this justice is to give to God 'that honour whiche is due to his divine majestie'. The Romans, says Elyot, honoured their gods by building great and noble temples, 'ordaynynge to them images, sacrifices, and other ceremonyes'. The Romans may have been pagans and mistaken about their gods, but their attitude was, in itself, not to be despised. They recognized the importance of rendering justice towards the divine; and the same may be said of Christian churches and ornaments dedicated to God. These things are necessary for the augmentation and continuing of reverence. Whether one follows Plato's opinion that all the world is a temple, or whether one believes that man is that temple, 'these materiall churches where unto repaireth the congregation of christen people, in the whiche is the corporall presence of the sonne of god and very god, aught to be lyke to the sayde temple, pure clene, and well adourned'. It is to illustrate how, by appropriate ceremonies, honour may be given where honour is due, that Elyot makes his observations concerning the coronation ritual.

The reason why Christian kings — even those who have succeeded by inheritance — receive their crowns and other regalia 'in an open and stately place before all their subjectes' is to impress in the hearts of the beholders 'perpetuall reverence, whiche is fountayne of obedience'. If this were not so, then kings might just as well be annointed privately, with less trouble both to themselves and to their ministers. It should also be considered, says Elyot, that 'we be men and nat aungels, wherfore we knowe nothinge but by outwarde significations'. The reward of virtue is honour which, with respect to kings, is expressed through the esteem of their subjects. This is not generally perceived 'but by some exterior signe, and that is either by laudable reporte, or excellencie in vesture, or other thinge semblable'. But, adds Elyot significantly, 'reporte is nat so commune a token as apparayle'. In olden times, he says, kings wore golden crowns; while the most noble Romans wore sundry garlands whereby their merit might be perceived. And the memory of this custom causes Elyot to return to the principal theme of his chapter with a lament over the folly of his contemporaries:

> O creatures moste unkynde and barrayne of Justyce that will denie that thinge to their god and creatour, whiche of very duetie and right is gyven to hym by good reason afore all princes, whiche in a degree incomparable be his subjectes and vassals. By which oppinion they seme to despoyle hym of reverence, which shal cause all obedience to cease, wherof will ensue utter confusion, if good christen princes meued with zeale do nat shortely provide to extincte utterly all suche opinions.

This fervent apology for ceremony and ornament has rich ideological implications for an England already witnessing the start of the debate concerning religious images and ritual, and which was soon to suffer the sort of iconoclastic fanaticism so deplored by Elyot. His remarks also have more general implications for Renaissance attitudes towards signs and symbols. Angels, he suggests, 'know' intuitively; whereas man — imprisoned in his body, and relying on physical sensations and laborious reasoning processes for his imperfect grasp of truth — can only know by 'outwarde significations'. Elyot is here making a straight-forward, but psychologically shrewd, observation on the way the human mind arrives at abstract conceptions through the medium of physical perception. To this extent he might be regarded as nudging towards a Neoplatonic theory of the function of the visual image.[2] But he does not venture that far, and we can only speculate about how he might have reacted to the more extreme iconoclasts who, having satiated their hatred of material idols in a frenzy of destruction, then sought to prevent even the private mental process of thinking in images, by probing into the very brains of Christian worshippers to excise the idols of the mind.[3]

Images and idolatry

Debate on the nature and function of images, both before and throughout the Tudor period, was waged principally within the context of Christian worship and more specifically in the light of the second of the Ten Commandments, forbidding the making of any graven image and the worshipping thereof. This commandment had caused trouble from the earliest days of Christianity but, in England, the issue came to a head with Wycliffe and his followers on the one hand and those who answered them on the other. Naturally, the adversaries were mainly concerned with paintings, sculptures and carvings in churches and the ways in which these were regarded by worshippers. Were these material objects really the means whereby the unlearned might be led towards God? This was the view regularly advanced by the defenders of images. 'What scripture conveys to clerks', wrote Walter Hilton in the fourteenth century, 'a picture is wont to exhibit to layfolk'. Images call back the wandering mind to spiritual and divine things, he added, 'because they arouse from vain and worldly thoughts to more intent and frequent meditation upon unseen things and the desire for them'. This kind of argument carried no weight with the Lollards who insisted that it was all a snare and a delusion. All images were idolatrous; they taught nothing but sin; and what Christians needed was the word of God, not man-made puppets and feigned representations of spiritual truths which were, by their very nature, unrepresentable (Owst 1961: 137−9).

These were standard attitudes: and the debate rarely achieved much beyond the exchange of dogmatic assertions and abuse. In the middle of the fifteenth century, however, there was one very sophisticated defence of images which explored the nature of pictorial representation in a remarkable manner. This was the work of Reginald Pecock, a clear-headed, imaginative and independent thinker who based his arguments upon a penetrating analysis of the relative merits of the different senses and of the ways in which human beings actually regard images and talk about them. His treatment of the problem transcends the immediate religious issues and carries implications for all figurative art.

Pictures and statues, says Pecock, are not usually regarded as gods. To so regard them, he agrees, would certainly be idolatrous: but nobody who has reached the years of discretion, 'and is passid childhode, and which is not a natural fool', ever considers these things other than as 'rememoratijf signes or mynding signs of God and of Seintis' (Pecock, ed. Babington 1860: I, 145, 148–9). This works in exactly the same way as portraits and statues of those whom we love, which help us to think about them more often and make them 'the more loved and the better served' (*op. cit.* 164). It is true that people often talk about images by name, but this does not mean that they believe the work of art to be, in fact, the person represented. The habit arises from the essentially figurative nature of human thought. When, for example, we visit our parish church and say, 'here lieth my fadir and there lieth my graunt fadir, and in the other side lieth my wijf', we know full well that the sepulchre contains nothing but bare bones. Or, if we see a painting or tapestry, we may say 'here ridith King Arthir, and there fightith Iulius Cesar, and here Hector of Troie throwith doun a knyt': but we certainly do not delude ourselves that these are live people on the wall or in the cloth. These are all 'figuratijf spechis' and their use is part of human nature (*op. cit.* 150–1). From the earliest times, Pecock points out, it has been customary for people to speak and write their words not only literally, 'in treuthe', but also to achieve effects, beauty and 'sum deliciosite'. These are 'certein colouris of rethorik' making discourse 'the more lusti', just as we use spices and sauces to make our meat 'the more savori and more plesant' (*op. cit.* 255). As for the use of images for religious purposes, says Pecock (anticipating Elyot's comment on the need for external significations), this is necessary because the mind of man is feeble and requires every aid possible. The act of reading a book is dependent upon the sense of hearing. It is a slow, laborious business even for the clerk and is immeasurably more so for an illiterate. By contrast, the sense of sight enables a matter to be grasped instantly and to be better retained. Pages of book learning can be conveyed by a single apposite image: by a story 'openli ther of purtreied or peintid in the wal or in a clooth'. The sense of sight 'schewith and bringith into the ymaginacioun and into the mynde withynne in the heed of a man myche mater and long mater sooner, and with lasse labour and traveil and peine, than the heering of the eere dooth'. Even a man who can read will grasp the gist of a story more speedily by sight, and with less labour and 'pein in his brayn', than by listening to other men's reading, or even by hearing his own reading. And, of course, this is even more true of those who are unable to read at all. They can never find men so ready to read a dozen leaves of a book to them as they shall find 'redy the wallis of a chirche peintid or a clooth steyned or ymagis sprad abroad in dyverse placis of the chirche' (*op. cit.* 209, 212–13)[4] Moreover, Pecock appreciated the psychological potency of pictorial symbolism. Not only did it offer a more rapid mode of comprehension, it also greatly enriched men's spiritual experience and, as Margaret Aston puts it, 'to deny such aids was to deprive every kind of believer, literate and illiterate alike, of an approach to God which few could afford to dispense with' (Aston 1988: 152).

The matter of this controversy did not greatly change in Tudor England. Indeed, the imaginative insights of Pecock seem to have been overlooked as, for the most part, the affair degenerated into violent, sterile and repetitive polemic, with the iconoclasts increasingly in the ascendant. What is of interest to us is the fact that, while it *should* have been difficult for the controversialists totally to avoid considering the signs and symbols of royalty, on the whole they simply funked it. Were all images, secular as well as sacred, to be condemned? And if not, what degree of respect should an image of royalty be accorded? If bowing before an idol was forbidden, what of offering some similar token of reverence to a royal portrait on a seal or the royal arms? The problems seem glaringly obvious: yet few writers even touched upon this theme; and those who did tended to be evasive, confused and irrelevant.

At about the time that Elyot included his little aside against iconoclasm in *The Book of the Governor*, the status of the royal image on the king's seal, and its relation to other images, had been briefly debated in *The examinacyon of William Thorpe*. Actually, the debate had taken place in 1407 when Thorpe, an eloquent follower of Wycliffe, had been rigorously examined on this and other matters by Thomas Arundel, Archbishop of Canterbury. As we can see from Elyot's remarks, the whole issue had become relevant again in 1530 or thereabouts, when *The examinacyon*, annotated by Tyndale, was put into print. Thorpe had maintained, very ambiguously, that although carvings, castings and paintings have been accepted by man and have been regarded as a 'calendar to lewd men, that neither can, nor will be learned to know God in his word, neither by his creatures, nor by his wonderful and divine workings', they should not be worshipped 'in form, nor in the likeness of man's craft'. Nevertheless, he added, 'every matter the painters paint with, since it is God's creature, ought to be worshipped in the kind, and to the end that God made and ordained it to serve man'. The Archbishop was not taken with this evasive rigmarole and declared:

> I grant well that nobody ought to do worship to any such images for themselves. But a crucifix ought to be worshipped for the passion of Christ that is painted therein, and so brought there-through to man's mind: and thus the images of the blessed Trinity, and of the virgin Mary, Christ's mother, and other images of saints, ought to be worshipped. For lo, earthly kings and lords, which use to send their letters ensealed with their arms or with their privy signet to men that are with them, are worshipped of

these men. For when these men receive their lords' letters, in which they see and know the wills and biddings of their lords they do off their caps to these letters. Why not then, since in images made with man's hand we may read and know many divers things of God and of his saints, shall we not worship their images.

Thorpe maintains that these worldly images of temporal lords may be used without sin: but he does not explain why and merely asserts that, in the light of biblical prohibitions uttered by Moses, David, Solomon, Baruch and others, this is 'no similitude to worship images made by man's hand' (Thorpe, ed. Christmas 1849: 94–5).

Even those who were sympathetic to pictures and sculptures in churches could do little better when trying to justify the respect due to royal images. An early writer on the Decalogue showed the normal direction followed in this aspect of the debate. Of course images are permissible for, he argues, did not 'the noble clerke Bede' point out that both Solomon in his temple and Moses in his tabernacle displayed 'dyverse peyntyngs and graves', and this by God's own commandment? And surely Christ, seeing the image of Caesar on a penny, would never have declared, 'yylde to Cesar thynges that beth his'. Rather he would have 'reprehended the ymage of Cesar, by cause of ydolatrie that myghte be to the image in a peny' (Owst 1961: 141–2). This story of Christ's exhortation to render tribute to Caesar was later used by Reginald Pecock for much the same purpose and, in his view, the episode demonstrates that Christ accepted that the Jews should 'have and use a graven ymage of the Emperour, as of her soverayn lord in erthe' (Pecock, ed. Babington 1860: 139–40).

Christ and the imperial coinage became the stock in trade not just for those who accepted images in churches but also for those who did not but still wished to avoid offending the monarch. John Hooper, for example, writing in 1547, in the middle of a long fulmination against every kind of image, suddenly and inconsequentially tells his reader that 'the art of graving and painting is the gift of God'. It is even tolerable to have the picture or image of any martyr, provided that it is not in the temple of God, nor otherwise abused. Christ by the 'picture of Caesar taught his audience obedience unto the civil prince, saying, *Cujus est haec imago? Caesaris, inquit. Ergo reddite quae sunt Caesari.* But if a man will learn to know God by his creatures, let him not say "Good morrow, master", to an old moth-eaten post,' (Hooper, ed. Carr 1842: 44–5). The argument does not advance us very far along the road of royal iconography. Nor do we get any further in the more elaborate discussion of the issue in Thomas Becon's *Catechism*, written early in the 1560s. Becon's treatment of the second Commandment consists principally of a violent attack on 'idle idols and mumming mawmets', and, in the course of this, he poses the question whether it is lawful for Christians to have images at all — that is out of church as well as in. 'There be some', says the catechized son to his catechizing father, 'that so think, of whose judgement I am not'. The Turks, he adds, do take this position and will not suffer any image to be made not even in 'profane and civil things'. Is it then lawful, demands the father, 'in politic, civil, and worldly matters to have images'? Well, replies the son, the story of Christ and Caesar's tribute shows that they are not forbidden in such worldly spheres: but they are absolutely intolerable in matters of godliness and religion. Furthermore, when dealing with the question of what is meant by bowing down unto an image, the son explains that this is 'reverently with the body to fall down before it, to kneel unto it, to set it in a place where we use to worship God, to garnish it with costly array and precious jewels, to kiss it, to put off our cap unto it, and to shew any gesture of reverence outwardly unto it'. All these things, he says, 'God doth forbid to be given to images in this his second commandment' (Becon, ed. Ayre 1844: 68–72).[5]

The thinness of this particular stretch of ice becomes clearer when we consider the position adopted by James Calfhill in his *Answer to John Martiall's Treatise of the Cross* (1565). For Calfhill, images and idolatry are inseparable. An image is a 'gay puppet', and it cannot be placed in a house of worship without serving as an 'allure to a wicked worship'. Experience and examples have shown us that 'Princes, for their pleasure erecting Images, have bred the vile affection of Idolatry'; and if the picture of a mere mortal creature 'be of such force to crook the soul' what then of images of saints and of Christ himself? This sort of thing, in Calfhill's opinion, was all right for heathens who did not believe in the immortality of the soul and 'were altogether vainglorious and proud'. They took pleasure in having their images set up, and their children 'rejoiced in their parents' folly'. They had no other reward for good deeds, and they had no laws forbidding such counterfeits: 'yea, the law itself, to excite men to virtue, decreed *Statuas in foro*, "Images in the market-place"'. Christians, however, have laws against such things in places of prayer.

> Wherefore I may say, with the good Fathers of Frankford 'if mortal men, puffed up with frowardness of their own vanity', proud of worldly pomp, bragging, ambitious, because they could not be in all places, would be magnified in some place; because they looked for no heavenly profit, would therefore have an earthly praise; shall this enforce us to make a Picture of our God, who is in every place ... He is not with colours to be pourtrayed. to be seen in temples made with man's hand, to be honoured or known in a beggarly Picture.
>
> (Calfhill, ed. Gibbings 1846: 358–9)

That this is a damning judgement not merely upon religious imagery but upon portraiture and sculpture in general is made apparent by Calfhill's next observation on the 'vain painter's or carver's craft' which, though it may delight men's fancies, has evil effects. Observe the example of Julius Caesar who, inspired by a fine portrait of Alexander the Great, grew ever more ambitious and was 'through a Picture made a plague of the world'; or Scipio Africanus who, by looking on his forefathers' monuments, had more occasion of pride than cause of praise given him.[6] Calfhill nevertheless concedes the possibility that — while, in relation to God, images are nothing other than the 'Devil's rhetoric' — in worldly affairs, 'for special policy', such things may be tolerable 'to keep in memory the noble facts of other', or to stir our affections with 'counterfeits of our absent friends'.

This concession to secular imagery is a grudging and graceless afterthought, wholly lacking in conviction. Similarly, the oft-reiterated references to Christ and the imperial coinage were largely irrelevant for they demonstrated nothing except that, since the coins were stamped with Caesar's head, these might legitimately be paid back to him as tribute. On this basis, secular portraiture served merely to identify an object — in this case a coin. Always in these discussions there remains the great hiatus: the carefully avoided question of what to do about images of monarchy whether in the form of seals, coins, portraits and, especially, the royal arms in which form they were increasingly finding their way into churches.[7]

Iconographic and ideological anomalies

When, in 1571, Archbishop Edmund Grindal published his various *Injunctions* and, amongst much else, ordered the destruction of altar stones and the taking down of crosses from the roodlofts, he stipulated that their place should be taken with 'some convenient crest' (Grindal 1571, ed. Nicholson 1843: 134). It is clear, from the fragmentary but considerable evidence still available to us, that it had become common to set up — in this exalted station — the royal arms; and those hostile to the Reformation in England had no doubt as to the significance of this development. The famous controversialist, Nicholas Sander, wrote:

> In the place of the cross of Christ, which they threw down, they put up the arms of the king of England, namely three leopards and three lilies, having for supporters the outstretched feet of a serpent and a dog. It was like a declaration on their part that they were worshippers, not of our Lord, whose image they had contemptuously thrown aside, but of an earthly king, whose armorial bearings they had substituted for it.
>
> (Sander, trs. Lewis 1877: 172)

The Anglican position on this issue, as on the whole question of royal imagery, was feeble and ill thought-out. One of the most striking aspects of the industry which developed quite early on in the reign of Elizabeth I, to manufacture and circulate portraits of the Queen, was its lack of a theoretical basis. That it was organized is evident.[8] What those involved considered to be its purpose is something which remains matter for conjecture. It has become customary now to talk about a *cult* of Elizabeth: yet it is by no means clear just what this might have meant to contemporaries.

Obviously, within the context of the debate concerning images, the position was extremely difficult as can be seen from the kind of evasiveness already cited. Consider also the hopeless discussion of the issue by one of the official apologists for the Church of England, Thomas Bilson (1585: 547—80). Bilson has a Jesuit man of straw raise the question why — since paying reverence to an image of an earthly prince is not deemed idolatrous — it *should* be considered idolatrous to revere an image of God. Bilson's Christian mouthpiece replies that these are very different matters. He concedes that, although 'the images of Princes may not wel be despited or abused, least it be taken as a signe of a malicious hart against the Prince', bowing the knee or raising the hand to the image of a Prince is 'flat and inevitable idolatrie'. The Jesuit persists in demanding why we may not offer some sign of reverence to an image of Christ just as 'you doe to the thrones and letters of Princes, when themselves be not present'; but he is refuted by an assertion that

> Princes can expect no more but a sober reverence due to their states, expressed by some decent gestures of the bodie, that others may behold it; and that to be yeelded chiefly to their persons, and secondly to their deputies, vicegerents and messengers, such as they shall use or allow to represent their power or to notifie their pleasures. In which case they that honour the Princes throne, scepter, seale, swoord, token or Image, honour not the thinges which they see, but the power that sent them.
>
> (Bilson 1585: 560)

The respect paid to coats of arms or the images set up by princes 'is accepted as rendred to their owne persons, when they can not otherwise be present in the place to receive it but by a substitute, or a signe that shal represent their state'. It is hard to see why, on this argument, something similar might not be said of religious objects. Indeed, it is precisely what *was* said by those who defended images. And it was also said when such thinkers accused the Anglican Church of replacing the worship of sacred Christian symbols with an idolatrous regard for the paraphernalia of kingship.

An interesting discussion of this problem, inspired by the recent spate of image-breaking in Portsmouth, occurs in a letter written by Stephen Gardiner to Captain Vaughan in May 1547 (Gardiner, ed. Muller 1933: 272−6). Gardiner believes that not only is iconoclasm an 'enterprise to subvert religion', it is also an attack on the 'state of the worlde' and especially on the nobility who use images to display publicly their lineage, parentage and 'remembrance of their state and acts'. This is, of course, an allusion to heraldic iconography; and Gardiner develops his argument by drawing attention to the way in which the royal arms are universally recognized. 'The pursivant', he writes, 'carieth not on his brest the Kinges names written in such letters as a few can spell, but suche as all can reade, be they never so rude, being greate knowen letters in images of three lyons, and three floures de luce, and other beastes holding those armes'. Moreover, Gardiner continues:

> he that cannot rede the scripture written about the Kinges great seale, either because he can not rede at al, or because the wax doth not expresse it yet he can reade Saint George on horsback on the one side, and the Kinge sitting in his majestie on the other side; and readeth so much written in those images, as if he be an honest man, he wil put of his cap. And although if the seale were broken by chaunce, he woulde and might make a candle of it, yet he would not be noted to have broken the seale for that purpose, or to cal it a pece of wax only whiles it continueth whole.

Gardiner's observations on the respect accorded to secular imagery are shrewd but, unfortunately, he made so catastrophic a blunder in his reading of the royal seal that the Protector Somerset, who undertook a reply, had no difficulty in ridiculing him. Yes, agreed the Protector, images may well be great letters: yet, as big as they are, there are many who read them amiss; and is it any wonder that lay people make mistakes when even Gardiner himself stumbles over a common image. The learned bishop has discovered St George on the King's great seal. But neither the picture, nor its accompanying inscription has anything to do with St George (see Fig. 2).

> As the inscription testifieth, the king's image is on both the sides; on the one side, as in war, the chief captain; on the other side, as in peace, the liege sovereign in harness, with his sword drawn, to defend his subjects; in his robes, in the seat of justice, with his

sceptre rightfully to rule and govern them, as he whom both in peace and war we acknowledge our most natural and chiefest head, ruler and governor.

In any case, adds Somerset, gleefully kicking his adversary when he is down, 'if it were S. George, my lord, where is his spear and dragon?

Fig. 2. Second Great Seal of Henry VIII. Engraving from Francis Sanford, *A Genealogical History of the Kings of England*, 1677, 457.

And why should the inscription round about tell an untruth, and not agree to the image?' (Foxe, ed. Townsend and Cattley 1837–41, VI: 28–30.)

Gardiner's ineptitude was especially unlucky not merely because it enabled Somerset to mock him but because it allowed the Protector to dodge the real point at issue. What was the status of the royal arms? Why should they be so respected? And, as these arms came to occupy an increasingly prominent place in churches, how did they differ from the images so reviled by the Reformers? As Nicholas Harpsfield jeered, in English churches, instead of the crucifix, you would now see, 'the arms of a mortal King set up on high with a dogg and a lyon, which a man might well call the abomination of desolation standing in the temple that Daniell speaketh of' (Harpsfield, ed. Pocock 1878: 282). And as for reverence and worship: well, said Nicholas Sander, 'Breake ... if you dare the Image of the Queenes Majestie, or the Armes of the realme'. Just pull down any banner, helmet, or other 'Ensigne or token' belonging to the honourable knights of the Garter or to any other worshipful order. 'If they take it well, then Christ may perhaps be content to see his owne Image destroyed.' (Sander 1567: fol.109^{r-v}.)

That the replacement of traditional Christian images in churches by displays of the royal arms signified the abolition of papal power and the exaltation of the Tudor monarchy must have been as obvious to contemporaries as it is to us. What is not at all obvious is the extent to which the royal arms could ever carry the same spiritual meaning, meet the same psychological needs, or elicit the same emotional response, as the cross or saintly relies had done. If they did not, then it is easy to believe that many ordinary folk would have shared the contempt expressed by Thomas Martin at Cranmer's examination: 'Down with the sacraments! Down with the mass! Down with the altars! Down with arms of Christ, and up with a lion and a dog!' (Cranmer, ed. Cox 1846: 217.) On the other hand, if they did, then they would have been as idolatrous as the images they had displaced.

The haphazard pragmatism of the Tudors – using images and retaining rituals when they suited a political purpose, and forbidding others when they did not – is particularly well illustrated by the history of the coin known as the angel and of the healing ceremony with which it was associated.[9] In 1465 Edward IV had introduced his angel which showed on the obverse a figure of St Michael trampling on the dragon which he transfixes with his spear. On the reverse is a ship with its mast in the form of a cross, surrounded by the legend, adapted from the Sarum Breviary, *Per Crucem tuam salva nos Christe Redemptor* (By your Cross save us, Redeemer Christ). St Michael was renowned as a healer of the sick: and it is very likely that this coin was minted as a touchpiece, or healing piece, for the King's Evil, to be awarded by the monarch on the various occasions set aside for charitable donation in the court year. Moreover the fact that angels were the only gold coins issued by Edward V and Richard III also suggests that they were especially minted for those monarchs and may have had a religious significance. It has been remarked by historians that all these rulers had political reasons for emphasizing the divine nature of their kingship, either by unction or heredity; and, during the Wars of the Roses, this question of the divine power to heal was much at issue. Fortescue, writing as a Lancastrian partisan between 1461 and 1463, asserted that the healing virtue belonged solely to Henry VI and denied it to Edward IV; and arguments such as these may have induced Edward to make his powers more widely known by the donation of angel touchpieces (Bloch 1973: 54−65).

This political motive was just as strong in the case of Henry VII who was careful to exploit every possible sanction to power and, although it has not been definitely established, it is likely that the special healing service of the English kings was instituted in his reign. In this service, the sick person, amidst prayers, was stroked by the monarch who crossed him with an angel touchpiece which was then hung about the patient's neck as an amulet 'until he be full whole'.[10] Whether or not Henry VII was involved with the institution of the healing service, there is ample evidence that he did undertake to touch for the King's Evil; and the resuscitation of this ancient ceremony, so closely bound up with the most sacred aspect of kingship, is a noteworthy element of Henry's concern with his public image. Fortescue had written that the gift of miraculous cures was a signal confirmation of an 'indubitable title' (Fortescue, ed. Clermont 1869: 70). A king who could heal was a king indeed.

It is not surprising, therefore, that Henry VIII should have continued with the healing and with the minting of angels as touchpieces − some of which are even marked with an annulet to indicate where the coins could be bored without defacing either the king's name or the head of the saint (Farquhar 1922: 41; Hocking 1906: I, no.826). Nor is it surprising that his daughter, Mary, retained the traditional thaumaturgy along with the angel, though with an altered legend. What is surprising is that the angel was minted under the extreme Protestant government of Edward VI, despite the contemporary attack on miracles, saints and old popish ceremonies. And more astonishing still is the survival of this miracle-working under Elizabeth I who exercised her therapeutic powers regularly as, for example, at the Kenilworth festivities of July 1575 when there were 'by her highnes accustumed mercy and charitee, nyne cured of the peynfull and daungerous diseaz, called the kings evill, for that the Kings and Queenz of this Realm withoout oother medsin (save only by handling and prayerz) only doo cure it' (Laneham, 1575 repr. 1969: 44–5). This is the best known occasion but, if William Clowes, one of the Queen's surgeons, is to be credited, Elizabeth cured constantly and copiously. In 1602 Clowes wrote that 'a mighty number of her Majestyes most Loyall subjects and also many strangers borne are daily cured and healed which otherwise would most miserably have perished' (Crawfurd 1911: 77).

The Elizabethan Office of healing is set out by Dr William Tooker in his treatise on the King's Evil, *Charisma: Sive Donum Sanationis* (1597). While the Chaplain reads the appropriate scriptural verse (Mark, XVI, 4):

> her most serene Majesty lays her hands on each side of them that are sick and diseased with the evil, on the jaws or the throat or the affected part, and touches the sore places with her bare hands, and forthwith heals them: and after their sores have been touched by her most healing hands the sick persons retire a while, while the rest of the ceremony is finished: then the Chaplain makes an end of the Gospel.

There follows a further reading by the Chaplain (John, II, 1); at which point the Queen rises and each person is led back singly to receive the special coin, 'bored and slung on a ribband'. She makes the sign of the cross on the diseased part; 'and so with a prayer for the health and happiness of each and with a blessing, they are bidden to retire a while till the rest of the gospel is finished'.[11] Naturally, Elizabeth, like her brother and sister, continued to mint the angel coins required in this ceremony, and they remained iconographically similar to earlier examples – that is with the ship of state, rose, and royal arms on the reverse, and the image of St Michael triumphing over the dragon on the obverse (see Fig. 3).

Both ceremony and imagery were wholly anomalous. Yet – while other, lesser acts of thaumaturgy, such as the curing of cramps, were happily abandoned – none of the Tudors, whatever their religious stance, was willing to forgo possession of so mystical a power as curing the King's Evil. The problem of consistency, like that posed by royal arms in churches, deference to royal portraits, and respect for royal seals, was never seriously confronted: though Tooker did try to establish that the healing power continued in the English monarchy, despite the espousal of Protestantism. He cites, as decisive evidence, the cure of a Roman Catholic prisoner who admitted that the Bull of excommunication had not deprived the Queen of her gift (Crawfurd 1911: 70). This is feeble and servile stuff from an undistinguished mind. But even so scathing an adversary of every kind of Catholic magic as Reginald Scot

Fig. 3. Angel coins: Henry VI to James I
(Hocking, nos.728, 757, 778, 781,
790, 815, 892, 929, 935, 950, 1042).

noted, in his *Discoverie of Witchcraft* (1584), the ability to cure the King's Evil:

> which hath beene alwaies thought, and to this daie is supposed to be a miraculous and a peculiar gift, & a speciall grace given to the kings and queenes of England. Which some referre to the proprietie of their persons, some to the peculiar gift of God, and some to the efficacie of words. But if the French king use it no woorse than our Princesse doth, God will not be offended thereat: for hir maiestie onelie useth godlie and divine praier, with some almes, and referreth the cure to God and to the physician.
>
> (Scot, ed. Nicholson 1886: 247)

This is disingenuous. Scot deliberately ignores the actual ceremony of touching; he writes as though the coins were donated as alms rather than used as amulets; and he omits the sign of the cross. Coming from the pen of perhaps the most sceptical English thinker of the sixteenth century, this account of monarchical miracle-working is a blatant prevarication.[12] In fact, the tension between magical rite and reformist zeal, as exemplified in royal thaumaturgy, did not become explicit until James I — with his Calvinist ministers breathing hotly down his neck — ascended the English throne. The scholarly and shrewd King had no faith in the ceremony and believed that, since the age of miracles was past, neither he nor any other king could heal scrofula. On the other hand, like his predecessor, he was reluctant to lose this prerogative which was so valued by his English subjects; and, in the end, he too persevered both with the touching ceremony and with the issue of angels (Crawfurd 1911: 82–9; Farquhar 1922: 65–72). As in other instances of rites and imagery, political prudence triumphed over both religious conviction and intellectual consistency.

Clement Urmeston and the talismanic royal image

It is clear that, while notions of an exalted monarchy (habitually manifested through magnificence, rituals, ceremonials, special apparel and regalia) were perfectly familiar in England during the fifteenth and sixteenth centuries, they did not amount to a general theory of the visual image as a hieroglyph of an individual ruler or a dynasty. Yet, in the mid-1530s, just as the debate concerning images was gathering momentum, there was one writer who did try to get to grips with the idea of using the royal image specifically both as talisman and as political propaganda.

Clement Urmeston, or Armstrong as he is often known to economic historians, began his career in London as an apprentice to the Grocers Company who admitted him as freeman in 1502.[13] Subsequently he must have switched interests, for his next appearance was at the Field of Cloth of Gold in 1520 where he was involved, along with John Rastell and John Browne the King's Painter, in decorating the 'large and stately' roofs of Henry VIII's temporary palace, and where he came under the special notice of the commissioners in charge of construction for his estimate involving 'a mervelous greate summe of monye' (Nichols 1846: 83−4). Like the other artists, he was also concerned with preparing the round theatre at Calais in 1520, and the theatre at Greenwich for the revels of May and November 1527; and, in each instance, his speciality was in providing antique wall illuminations, chandeliers and 'dawnsing lights' − hanging wickerwork human figures bearing torches. In 1530 he turned up at Esher and York Place working on Wolsey's houses; and he supplied garnishings for the roof of the new gallery at Westminster Palace in 1532 when he is described as a joiner. Then suddenly, with the onset of the Henrician Reformation and the break with Rome, Urmeston plunged his pen deep into the inkpot and started to write long, rambling socio-economic, politico-religious treatises which he submitted to Thomas Cromwell, setting forth 'the knowledge of the right order of commen weale of all peple in the Realme', so that Cromwell could help the King establish it as an example to all other realms.[14]

The most complete, though characteristically incoherent, exposition of Urmeston's theories remains buried in an autograph volume entitled *Sermons and declaracions agaynst popishe ceremonyes* (Public Record Office MS.E.36/197). Here he sets out his idiosyncratic view of the royal office, and attempts to provide Cromwell with a novel means for consolidating the Reformation. The laws of God, he writes, are in the form of 'light of sonne and moone and sters over all laws in this world' (*op. cit.* 59). For Urmeston the sun is the central point of the universe. It is the point between the earthly man and the heavenly man: that is between the laws of God, first taught to Adam by faith, and the laws of this world which were made by man's reason and have prevailed since Adam's sin. Now the King has mystic qualities bestowed upon him by the holy unction. He is an earthly man with the ability to rise above earthly things when, being inwardly moved by the grace of God, he can not only understand the heavenly laws but also can help apply them in this world. The ordinary people have to work for their daily meat, but this *living* − that is literally food and labour − does not come as a gift directly from God but must be provided by the King who should lead his people to material, and thence to spiritual, well-being. The King must see himself to be, 'a right hedd lorde in godd to giff lyvynge to all his peple and must owt of erthly man rise into the hevynly man in spirit above the sone to giff to all his peple lyvynge wher god gevyth theym levynge'.

One can clearly see the way in which Urmeston's social and economic theory derives from his mystic conception of kingship. The King is the head of the body politic, with his advisers, lords, knights and esquires growing out from beneath his shoulders as 'armes handes and fyngers' just as these limbs are part of an earthly man's body (*op. cit.* 99).[15] All these parts must work together for the common weal; and there are, in the main, two sorts of labour necessary − husbandry and 'artificialitie'. Unfortunately, there are some people who have striven for riches without considering the common good and, in particular, Urmeston attacks lawyers whose wealth derives from people's distress and the prior commitment of sin, and merchants who make their money out of scarcity while carrying riches out of the kingdom (*op. cit.* 98).[16] The common weal has thus decayed, because many people do not have labour and 'levynges' given to them but are forced to do the best they can on their own. It is the King's task to supply this need and so lead his people away from earthly sin.

Urmeston is very confused both in his corporeal and astronomical metaphors for the common weal. The sun, as well as being the point between earthly and heavenly things, is also God's great 'brode seale of his rigt of marcy, that is the sonne *sol justitie* the ligt of this world'. Just as the sun is the head among the heavenly bodies, giving light and life to earthly things, so the King is the 'sone of man' with his dual position symbolized in his 'hedde seale' − the image of the King's body being in this world but with his head in the heavens and in God's laws (*op. cit.* 66−8).[17] To make this figure clear, Urmeston draws on the story of Saul, first king of Israel, who was 'from the shulders upwards hygher than all the peple'.[18]

This brings Urmeston to what he believed to be one of his most important suggestions to aid the Reformation. The King's mystic significance is expressed in his 'hedde seale' − that is, literally, a seal with the royal head depicted thereon − and in this, 'the forme of goddes laws shalbe present with his own persone wher so ever he goo and rule, signyfieng he hath the grace of god with hym anoyntid with goddes holy spirit'. From this great seal there should be lesser seals for the 'hedd howsis over all bodies of shires'. All these, suggests Urmeston, must seal in wax for recording the causes of 'rigth of the Reame'; and from them are to be sent out lesser 'hedd sealis' to the head houses of every parish and cure within the Church: 'which seale shalbe prynt parchement and paper with ynke of litle charge'. Every householder is to have such a seal in parchment every Easter and is to keep it with him for the whole year 'wher so ever he ride or goo, to Record with hym how he lyvith in Cure'. Only servants and others who are not householders will be without these seals: but even they must live under the cure of those who do possess them. Since man's sin nobody is able to receive the gift of grace from God, but must receive it from the

King, God's minister, whose powers and heavenly office are represented in the seal which thus, in Urmeston's view, combines an almost magical, talismanic value with the function of an identity card authenticating its bearer's loyalty (*op. cit.* 71−2).

Urmeston was especially keen that the King himself should be aware of his own mystic powers and exceptional privileges. And there was a very practical reason behind this desire. The King, Urmeston asserts, has been so blinded by the teaching of man and by earthly laws that he has been vexed and troubled more than all the other kings of Christendom in the outlay of the riches of his realm for the Pope's maintenance. Something in excess of three million pounds, 'oon weys and an other', has been spent in this way. Moreover, the people have been disturbed by the Pope and his minions whose laws are inconsistent and hostile to the King's spiritual powers which they claim for themselves. They say that they are the lords of the bodies and the souls of all people but, argues Urmeston, the Pope's laws are of this world under the sun; and one cannot put away sin by the application of laws which arise from that sin. The King, therefore, should take all the souls and bodies of his people into his own cure because the Pope has failed to make the people better inwardly despite cloaking his wickedness with an appearance of holiness − the cloak 'therof is an old dispisid foule bawdy cote, shamfully araied and spottid with syne' (*op. cit.* 92). Yet, if this vile garment is removed, the people will think themselves to be stark naked unless the King demonstrates his ability to undertake the cure of his subjects. The Pope is not without support for his claims. The Emperor, with his vast accretion of territories, is in league with him; and together they are determined that there must never be a general council in which the realms of Christendom could take Christ as their head lord.

The Pope claims to be head of the Church, but this is really the King's position. And here Urmeston parallels his view of the significance of the royal seal by developing an interesting extension of medieval architectural symbolism. Arguing from an identification of the cruciform church with the figure of man, Urmeston maintains that the head part of a church is the choir and that this represents the kingly office. But the Pope and his ministers have taken away the choir from all churches and so destroyed the head office of Christian kings. Presumably he is here thinking of the chancel screen which did, literally, cut off the choir from the main body of the church and thus, to the writer's way of thinking, severed the King from his subjects (*op. cit.* 90−1). It is up to the King to assert his own authority which is God's law; and Urmeston advocates that this should be done without any argument or explanation. The King should simply take all his subjects into his 'Cure' and should 'leif not oon Soll to liff under no cure of the popes law' (*op. cit.* 108).

The bases for Urmeston's political theory are obviously, in the first instance, biblical and he quotes frequently from both the Old and the New Testament. More generally, the comparison or identification of kingship with the rule of the sun in the heavens has a history dating back to remote antiquity:[19] but it is impossible to say precisely how Urmeston formed his ideas or whence they were derived. We are rather better informed about what became of them for they ended up, metaphorically if not literally, in Thomas Cromwell's wastepaper bin. Indeed, the old artist felt obliged to write to the minister complaining, 'rigt sory have I been that your mastership wold never Inwardly see and know the Image of the kyng upberyng upon his shulders the chirch of crist in his hevynly manhed, which is signyfied in an ordinary Seale of his hedd office' (Pauli 1878: 48).

Urmeston even addressed some of his effusions to Henry himself.[20] But he was simply ignored; and it is not difficult to understand why. The busy minister would hardly have had the time and energy necessary to disentangle Urmeston's confusingly argued and wildly scrawled treatises; and doubtless Cromwell, like his modern admirer Professor Elton, would have deemed them nothing but 'repetitive and flatulent rhapsodies' (Elton 1973: 112). Yet this was a pity because Urmeston's suggestion, imaginatively handled, might have been an effective mode of mediating between the high falutin Caesaro-papism of Henry's learned apologists and a wider, ill-educated public. Certainly, Urmeston was the only sixteenth-century Englishman to have left record of a fully developed theory concerning the political potency of the royal image.

The cosmic schemes of Clement Urmeston which, as far as we can tell, were unique in England, and the views of the controversialists, whose arguments about images and idolatry were commonplace, suggest the limits of Tudor iconographic theory. There was, however, another quite different approach to personal imagery which proved both more effective and more enduring.

From heraldic badge to dynastic hieroglyph

Henry Tudor — addressing his first parliament in November 1485, less than three months after his victory at Bosworth — declared that his right to the throne was based on just inheritance and on the judgement of God given in battle.[21] The latter was the more effective claim: but the former was to provide the basis for Tudor dynastic mythology and its visual expression. The matter was primarily genealogical; the manner in which genealogy was customarily advertised was essentially, though not exclusively, heraldic; and anyone seeking expert guidance on genealogy and heraldry was likely to turn, in the first instance, not to philosophers and political theorists, but rather to Garter King of Arms and his fellow officers. And these heralds had their own rich iconographic traditions and lore which owed little to the neo-classical fancies of the erudite.

By the latter half of the fifteenth century the functions of the heralds, their records and their special skills had become clearly defined; and the authority of the officers of arms continued to be recognized despite the personal idiosyncrasies, conflicting ambitions and squabbles which marked their activities throughout the Tudor period. Their armorial expertise had developed, along with increasing heraldic complexity, into a virtual monopoly. The days when a barber might identify the banners of an opposing army for his master, as did Simon de Montfort's at Evesham in 1265, had long since passed. Indeed, the barber's efforts were no recommendation for amateurism since his blunders had precipitated Simon's downfall (Walter of Hemingburgh, ed. Hamilton 1848: 323). The heralds were professionals. They knew about arms; and, even if they had not themselves invented the esoteric language and symbolism in which these were couched, they certainly developed and perpetuated them.[22] The heralds drew up and preserved the rolls on which arms were recorded; and they had grown accustomed to having such materials ready to hand in their own archives to serve both as checks and as precedents.

The custody of these records was one important factor embittering the relations between Thomas Wriothesley (Garter) and Thomas Benolt (Clarenceux) in 1530. Garter knew perfectly well, said Benolt, that there was a house appointed where the heralds had 'there studdes and lernynges wherein lay all there bookes of the offyce of Armes & all such constitucions actorytes & privileges graunted & geven to the sayde offyce of Armes by ryght noble princes in tymes past'. Both house and library had been in the keeping of Garter's father, Sir John Writhe, who, when the house was taken from the heralds, had improperly retained the books and transferred them to his own dwelling. His son now kept them for his 'singuler use weale & profette' and was thus able to defy any other officer of arms 'to bryng forth any actorytes agaynst hym' (Wagner 1956: 94). This may have been a serious inconvenience, though Benolt should have been able to hold his own comfortably in any combat waged with precedents, for the inventory of his own library is an impressive document. It lists some fifty-four manuscript books or sheets, seventeen rolls of pedigrees, seven rolls of arms, thirteen narrative or record rolls, and twenty-three historical, military and miscellaneous printed books: while, amongst these heraldic treasures were, very significantly, eleven paper rolls bound together in one bundle 'wherof ys mynutes and greves of all the office of armes against Garter' (Wagner 1956: 151–7, 1967: 171; Dennys 1975: 55–8).

The heralds had first risen into prominence with the development of the tournament, and increasingly became associated with spectacle and state ritual.[23] By 1485, when they received letters of incorporation from Richard III, they were acknowledged masters of ceremony both in the practical sense of organization, and as makers and custodians of written records. There is, moreover, scattered but decisive evidence from the reign of Henry VII onwards that the heralds were responsible for preparing pictorial records of significant state occasions. The most famous of these are the 18 metre vellum roll depicting scenes from Henry VIII's Westminster tournament of February 1511, and the 7 metre roll showing the procession to Parliament just one year later.[24] But as early as 1487 a herald, discussing the creation of Knights of the Bath at the coronation of Elizabeth of York, refers to the 'Maner and forme as the Picture thereof shewethe'; and a version of this record survives in one of the manuscripts which John Writhe, Garter King of Arms at the time, bequeathed to his son. There must also have been illustrations of the coronation procession itself: for the herald refers to 'the Book of Picture therof made'.[25] Possibly these constituted another series similar to those for the Knights of the Bath; or they may have been thumbnail sketches like those surviving for the baptism of Edward VI in 1536, the funeral of Anne of Cleves in 1557, or the coronation of Elizabeth I in 1559 — all of which were clearly intended to serve as a pictorial supplement and clarification of written narratives (see Fig. 4).[26]

The heralds were custodians of genealogical knowledge; they were specialists in the science of armory whereby genealogy was visually represented; and, although the administrative mechanisms whereby their skills were harnessed to the needs of public image-making remain difficult to describe, there were two occasions in the reign of Henry VIII which are very revealing of the ways in which they were consulted. In one of the letters written by the English commissioners at the Field of Cloth of Gold, complaining about the 'greate and importunate charges' of the work being carried out by Clement Urmeston and his colleagues, there is a request that Cardinal Wolsey should command 'Gartyr the king of heraudes, that he by th'advise of all the other the kings heraudes, do make a boke in picture of all the armes, . . . bestes, fowles, devises, badges and congnisances of the kinges highnes, the quenes grace, the Frenche king . . . the dolphin and the princes dothe bere' (see Fig. 5) (Nichols 1846: 83). Unfortunately, despite the mass of material relating to the Anglo-French interview, we would know nothing about the heraldic decoration were it not for one meticulous eye-witness, Elis Gruffudd, who informs us that all the walls throughout the English temporary palace were hung with priceless tapestries above which was a 'painted border of carvers' work filling the space between

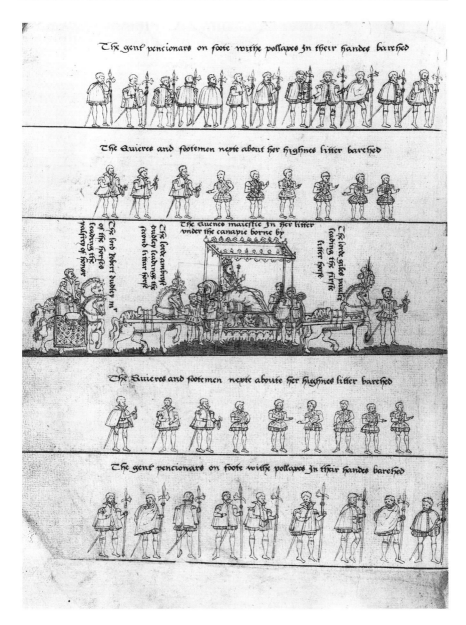

Fig. 4. Heraldic pen drawing of Queen Elizabeth I in procession. College of Arms MS. M.6, fol.41ᵛ. For a detail of this page, see Fig. 24 below.

Fig. 5. Jousting cheque for the Field of Cloth of Gold in June 1520 (Society of Antiquaries MS). This remains an enigma. Obviously intended as part of a presentation volume — with its selection of armorial shields and the arms of France and England enclosed respectively within the collars of St Michael and St George — it records only a few scores from the ten days of tilting and does not cover any of the many periods when the two kings performed.

the hangings and the ceiling'. On this border were images of classical figures 'holding the armorial bearings of the ancestors of various kings and princes in their hands', all carved in the 'most perfect manner imaginable'.[27] Given the prodigious size of the building and the great number of apartments it contained, providing the detail for this armorial frieze must have been the principal work undertaken by Garter and his associates for the Field of Cloth of Gold.[28] We do not have a similar request for heraldic advice relating to the temporary theatre built at Calais for the entertainment of Henry VIII and the Emperor Charles V immediately after the Anglo-French interview. But it is certain that the heralds were again involved, because the entrance and vestibule of the theatre were filled with a series of statues each bearing a shield of arms relevant to Henry, Charles and their territories. Within the theatre there were 'plusieurs nouveaultez' including, on each of the first thirteen pillars of the gallery, two armorial shields and devices relating to the monarchs, their wives and the orders of the Garter and the Toison d'Or; and on the rest of the pillars were the arms of 'seigneurs, princes, grans maistres sans devises'.[29]

The heralds' knowledge of imperial armory was again tested in 1522 when a pageant series was prepared in London for the entry of Charles V. On 8 May 1522 there was recorded in the *Repertories* of the City of London an agreement that 'the chamberlyn shall geve unto Master Garter kyng of haroldes for such payne and labor that he now takys with devysyng of the pageauntes and other thynges agenst the comyng of themperor in to the Citie v. marcs' (*Repertories* IV, fol.117ᵛ). There is no other specific allusion to Garter's work, but the results of his labour are patent, for shields of arms and genealogies formed a prominent feature of the series.[30] The first pageant at London Bridge showed a table of all the Emperor's lands, and the bridge itself was adorned with 'Targettes of the Armes of the Emperour and his Dominions richely paincted'. The second pageant celebrated the feats of Jason – honouring the Order of the Golden Fleece of which the Emperor was head – and must have included appropriate heraldic decoration, though no details have survived. The third pageant displayed the arms of the Electors of the Empire; and the fourth, prepared by the Italian merchants resident in London, consisted of a genealogical tree showing, in detail, the joint descent of Henry and Charles from John of Gaunt. The fifth was a castle with two towers, 'set with vanes and scutions of the armes of the Emperor and the kyng'; and between the towers was a palace of King Arthur surrounded by the noble princes over whom he ruled. 'all bearyng Targettes of their armes'. The galleries of the seventh pageant were filled with 'Targettes and scutchions of the Emperors and kynges arms and devises', as was the eighth which depicted the joint descent of the monarchs from Alphonso the Wise of

Castile who reclined at the foot of the scene with a genealogical tree growing out of his breast. On this tree sat many kings, queens and princes: 'lively persones richly appareled every one with a scutchion of armes shewyng their mariages, and in the highest braunche satte the Emperor, the kyng and just v. and vii. degrees from the sayd kyng of Spayne' (Hall, ed. Ellis 1809: 639).

How 'lively' were these royal and noble figures? It is just possible that the reigning monarchs and their immediate forebears were recognizable: but there can have been no attempt at verisimilitude in the descendants of John of Gaunt and Alphonso of Castile because there were no authentic portraits of any of them; and realism would have been impossible in the case of King Arthur's vassals, since most of them had never existed. Not that this mattered. The face of the famous King Arthur, for example, might just as well have been a crowned circle – with two dots and a line for eyes and mouth – provided that he bore an argent cross on a green shield with, in the first quarter, the Virgin holding the child all gold (Dennys 1975: 47, 104, 201 note 46; Jones 1943: 89, 207). Similarly, the heralds knew no better than the artists of 1520 and 1522 what the vast majority of French and imperial princes looked like, but they could discover what was necessary by searching through records like those listed in Benolt's inventory. In fact, Benolt himself might have browsed through his copy of a book written in French by the mid-fifteenth-century herald, William Whiting, 'of popes emperours & kings of Englond with the armes of divers gentilmen painted'; or a 'booke concernyng many notes necessary for officers of armes writyn in frenche with divers noble mens armes of the reaulme of Fraunce'; or 'a booke of all the armes of Highe Almain painted'; or another of 'armes of divers gentilmen of beyonde see' (Wagner 1956: 151, 154).

Statues or paintings might look like anyone, or no one, provided that their arms and badges were correct. Many rolls of arms are illustrated by figures which purport to represent real people but, in fact, resemble only each other so that they are differentiated solely by their coats of arms. Even more striking is the roll depicting the procession to Parliament in 1512 where the faces of the King and his lords spiritual and temporal are interchangeable. Their arms, on the other hand, are not. A ruler, actually present in the flesh, might be recognized by his position in relation to those about him and, above all, by the splendour of his apparel. However, an absent ruler was identified not by physiognomy but by armorial ciphers; and this was especially the case when dynastic portraiture was rare, and where there was no systematic attempt to disseminate accurate representations of the royal face.

Henry VII came to the throne as representative of the House of Lancaster. In part this was because he could claim descent from John of Gaunt, third son of Edward III – a line, genuine though distant, which was traced through Henry's mother Margaret Beaufort and was acknowledged by the adoption of the portcullis which had long been a badge of the Beaufort family, and of the greyhound which likewise had Beaufort resonances (see Fig. 6).[31] Even more significant, however, was the fact that the greyhound had been favoured by Edward III and his Lancastrian heirs, and had been granted as an heraldic supporter by Henry VI to his half-brother, Edmund Tudor, when the latter was created Earl of Richmond. The greyhound became a favourite Tudor royal beast and was regularly used as a supporter of their royal arms; while the importance of the portcullis, which also became a common badge of the dynasty, was indicated when, in the early years of his reign, Henry VII created a new pursuivant with that title.[32] Henry had already created another pursuivant during his coronation celebrations and his title, *Rouge Dragon*, alludes to the King's descent, both through his mother and father, from the ancient Welsh princes (Anglo 1969: 14). The red dragon was a widely known symbol of the *British* monarchy, and it, too, was used as an heraldic supporter by all the Tudors and, like the portcullis, became a favourite Tudor device: though neither of these was quite as ubiquitous as the union rose which symbolized the marriage of Henry Tudor as Lancastrian heir to Elizabeth, Edward IV's daughter.[33]

These beasts and badges were all allusions to the Tudor descent or marriage: but very quickly they became symbols not of pedigree but of the dynasty itself. This distinction is crucial. The dynastic hieroglyphs of the Tudors were neither complicated nor subtle; they were straightforwardly heraldic: and they were, for this reason, especially effective. The whole point of badges was that they could be immediately recognized; and the portcullis, rose, dragon and greyhound appear on all things Tudor, both animate and inanimate. They marked a man as a royal servant − from the humblest household retainer with a badge on his cap to the most lofty Garter Knight whose golden chain was ornamented with double roses.[34] The Tudor badges are on seals and coins; in the borders and ornaments of manuscripts; on designs for royal pavilions; on plates, armour and cannon. They even adorned chamber-pots and close-stools. Above all they proliferated in chapels and palaces. But wherever, or on whomsoever, they appeared they were no merely decorative cosmetic. They always indicated proprietorial rights. And this was especially obvious with property which had belonged to someone else as when, for example, the *tapisser*, Cornelius van de Strete, was employed to weave red roses and portcullises into the borders of nine old tapestries; or when Quentin Poulet and his team of artists overpainted illuminations and added Tudor emblems to old manuscripts already in the royal collection; or when some unknown craftsman added a band of gold, coarsely decorated with applied Tudor roses in red and white enamel, to the fourteenth-century 'Royal Gold

A Sergeant at Armes

The Standerd of the Greyhound borne by m͞r Herbot brother to the Earle of Pembr

Yeomen Servitors in

Fig. 6. Standard of the Greyhound from the funeral procession of Elizabeth I. British Library MS. Additional 35,324, fol.30ʳ.

Cup of the Kings of France and England'. The tapestries, manuscripts and gold vessel were thus transformed into *Tudor* objects; just as King's College Chapel at Cambridge was transformed into a wholly Tudor chapel by being covered with heraldic marks of ownership (see Fig. 7).[35]

These were not trivial matters. Every time that Henry VIII changed his queen or took over the dwelling of some demoted unfortunate, arms, beasts and badges had to be adjusted accordingly, even though this meant not only new painted decorations but also new glass. In 1533–4, for example, there was a general expunging of Katharine of Aragon's arms which were replaced by those of Anne Boleyn. In their turn, Anne's leopards, which appeared at Hampton Court for a brief spell, were soon metamorphosed into Jane Seymour's panthers by 'new makyng of the hedds and the taylls'. Katharine Howard was queen when Henry converted the monastic buildings at Rochester into a royal house, and her arms and badges were promptly set up in the windows. But they only remained there for a couple of years before 'the takyng owte of the lady Haywards armys' was necessitated by her disgrace. It is not surprising, in view of the rapid turnover rate of Henry's infatuations and enthusiasms, that errors sometimes crept in. So Wolsey's arms still

Fig. 7. Tudor badges from King's College Chapel, Cambridge.

linger here and there at Hampton Court; heraldic vestiges of Anne Boleyn were never completely obliterated at St James and King's College Chapel; and even Anne of Cleves clings resolutely to the ceiling of the Chapel Royal despite the fact that it must have taken the painters longer to execute the appropriate arms, mottoes and ciphers than it took Henry to untie the matrimonial knots (Colvin 1963−82: IV, ii, 26−7, 104−5, 133−5, 242).

Of all the objects which heraldic imagery indelibly stamped as belonging to a specific dynasty, quite the most significant was the throne itself. Badges and devices loomed large in the political verse spawned by the internecine wars of the fifteenth century, and they continued to offer rich fare for political prognosticators under the Tudors.[36] At one stage things reached such a pitch that an Act of Parliament was considered necessary to deal with the problem, and in 1542 it was made a felony for any person to 'prynte or wryte, or elles speake sing or declare' prophecies relating to the King or to any other person, based upon an interpretation of 'Armes feldes beastes fowles or other suche lyke thinges accustomed in armes cognisaunces badges or signetes, or by reasone of lettres of the name of the King or of any other persone'[37] This was the result of popular meddling in the armorial aspect of affairs of state and it was far less dramatic than the case of Henry Howard, Earl of Surrey, whose heraldic vainglory led to his indictment and condemnation on a charge of high treason in 1546−7. Several years earlier, it had been noted that Surrey's arms were very similar to the King's; but the affair grew more serious when, in August 1546, Surrey had called Christopher Barker, Garter King of Arms, to his home in Lambeth and displayed 'a scocheon of the arms Brotherton and St Edwarde and Anjoye and Mowbreye quartered, and said he would bear it'. When questioned as to his title, Surrey answered that the arms were born by Brotherton − which the herald denied, saying that 'it was not in his pedigree'. The Earl insisted that he had found it in a house in Norfolk 'in stone graven so, and he would bear it'; and Garter, try as he might, could not dissuade him (Brewer *et al.* 1862−1932: XXI.i, no.1425).

There were several possible charges which could have been brought against Surrey. According to some depositions he had suggested that his sister, the Duchess of Richmond, should vamp the King and, by becoming his mistress, come to rule him. Other witnesses deposed that he had spoken harshly about the King's ministers; had suggested that his father, the Duke of Norfolk, should govern the heir to the throne in the event of Henry's death; and had maintained dubious communication with foreigners such as the French ambassador, Marillac (Brewer *et al.* 1862−1932: XXI.ii, no.555). Late in December 1546 Wriothesley, Henry's Chancellor, drew up a series of questions to serve as the groundwork for charges against the Howards in a document annotated by the King himself. Henry's hand was tremulous; his hatred inexorable; and the opening paragraphs illuminating.

> If a man cummyng of the colaterall lyne to the heyre off the crowne, who ought not to beare the Armes of England but on the second quarter, with the difference of there auncestre, doo presume to chaunge his right place, and beare them in the first quarter, leaving out the true difference of thauncestre, and in the lieu therof, use the very plase only of the Heire Masle Apparant; how thys mans intent is to be be juggyd; and whether this importe any daunger, peril, or slaundre to the title of the Prince, or very Heire Apparant; and howe it wayeth in our lawes.
>
> If a man presume to take into his armes an olde cote of the Crown, whyche hys awnceter never bare, nor he of ryght owght to bear, and use it without difference; whither it maye be to the peril or slaundre of the very Heire of the Crown, or to be taken to tende to his disturbaunce in the same; and in what peril they be, that consent that he shuld soo doo.
>
> (Royal Commission 1830–52: I.ii, 891)

In the end, the Bill of indictment concentrated entirely on the armorial issue, interpreting Surrey's use of arms and ensigns which were appropriate only to the King and his heir apparent as treasonable within the definition of the Act of 1537 (28 Henry VIII, cap.7, para.12) (Brewer *et al.* 1862–1932: XXI.ii, no.697). This had enacted that whosoever, by words, printing, or other external act, maliciously procured anything to the peril of the King's person or gave occasion whereby the King or his successors might be disturbed in their possession of the Crown, should be guilty of high treason. There was no lack of pretexts to bring Surrey to the block, yet, as Kenneth Pickthorn neatly summarized the situation: 'the treason that could be expounded to the public, that had no popular echo and yet was not too metaphysical to reach the popular ear, was the heraldic'.[38] To us it may seem curious and arbitrary to cut off a man's head because he displayed 'asur a crosse flewry betwene five merlettes golde' and conjoined with them 'thre labelles sylver'. To contemporaries the charge was viewed quite differently, and Surrey was condemned precisely because the shield of arms was said to belong solely to the King, and the three labels reserved for the heir apparent. Whether or not Surrey had a serious entitlement to the arms was irrelevant. The heralds had declared against him; the King felt threatened and malevolent; and − above all − the heraldic indictment was deemed, and proved, sufficient. For a nobleman to arrogate the royal arms, as Surrey was alleged to have done, was to make a bold and dangerous political statement. This was the one iconographical tradition which really mattered.

Chapter Two

THE *BRITISH HISTORY* AND ITS IMPLICATIONS[39]

When Henry VII visited Worcester in May 1486, during his first royal progress, the civic authorities, deeply mindful of their city's implication in the abortive Stafford insurrection, devised a short pageant series which judiciously mingled praise of the new monarch with pleas for mercy. For some reason the speeches were never delivered, but they survive in a detailed report written by a herald accompanying the King. Henry was to have been greeted at the city gates by a figure, *Janitor*, whose speech was a clever series of variations on the traditional theme of the Nine Worthies. Is the visitor Noah returning from the flood, asks *Janitor*; is it Jason with the golden fleece; or Julius Caesar 'with the Triumphe of Victorie'? Then, growing in confidence, *Janitor* abandons this interrogatory stance and identifies Henry with a series of biblical heroes — Abraham, Isaac, Jacob, Joseph and David — who had each suffered persecution or exile before returning to take possession of their rightful inheritance. Finally, via a classical detour, *Janitor* homes in on the visitor's true identity:

> Welcome Scipio, the whiche toked Hanyball.
> Welcome Arture, the very Britain Kyng.
> Welcome Defence to England as a Walle.
> Cadwaladers Blodde lynyally descending,
> Longe hath bee towlde of such a Prince comyng.
> Wherfor Frendes, if that I shal not lye,
> This same is the Fulfiller of the Profecye.
> (Leland 1770: IV, 196)

The issue here is the Welsh descent of Henry VII whose grandfather, Owen Tudor, came from an ancient family in Anglesey and could trace his descent via Llewellyn ap Griffith back to Cadwalader, and beyond. This may not seem much of a claim to the English throne: but the lineage had historical and emotional implications which were alluded to by *Janitor* at Worcester and which continued to attract attention until the death of Prince Arthur in 1502.

The heart of the matter lay in fifteenth-century attitudes towards the early history of Great Britain. These derived from the work of the twelfth-century mythographer Geoffrey of Monmouth whose *Historia Regum Britanniae* first linked together the elements which were to become familiar to generations of chroniclers, poets and politicians: the Trojan descent of the British kings; the prophecy to Cadwalader of an ultimate British triumph over the Saxon invaders; the mighty deeds of King Arthur; and the British significance of the red dragon.[40]

Geoffrey records the arrival of Brutus, grandson of the Trojan hero Aeneas, who — having conquered the giants then in possession of the land — went on to build a new Troy (Trinovantum), otherwise known as London. The realm was divided at Brutus's death but subsequently descended in the line of his eldest son; and several of these later kings gained considerable victories on the Continent even against Rome itself. However, a less happy era began with the Saxon invasions. The struggle against these newcomers led to the prophecies of Merlin and to a vision conjured up before King Vortigern of a tremendous battle between a red dragon, symbolizing the British, and a white dragon, symbolizing the Saxons. The red dragon, though initially getting the worst of the fight, eventually emerged the winner and thus presaged the final triumph of the British.

The *Historia* then proceeds to the varied fortunes of the following period which includes the deeds of the mighty King Arthur who not only overthrew the Saxons, Picts and Scots, Ireland, Iceland, Sweden, the Orkneys, Norway and Denmark, but also conquered Gaul and defeated a great Roman army which had attempted to halt his advance. Sadly, just as Arthur was preparing an assault upon Rome itself, news of rebellion forced him to return to Britain where he perished in the ensuing civil war. Finally, the land was overcome by the Saxons; and Cadwalader, the last British king, his resources drained by famine and plague, took refuge abroad and died at Rome. Then, as the book draws to its close, there is a restatement of the prophecies made to Vortigern — this time expressed by an angel who informs Cadwalader that the British would one day recover their land from the Saxons.

The impact of this historical farrago was astonishing, despite immediate challenges to its veracity. Both Giraldus Cambrensis and William of Newburgh expressed strong criticism. Yet their scepticism was drowned amidst a general tide of acceptance, and even those who, like Ralph Higden, were inclined to find fault with certain aspects of Geoffrey's narrative, were still prepared to accept the basic Trojan history scheme underlying it. They even adorned it with inventions of their own so that the *British History* became, in Kendrick's phrase, a 'formidable deadweight of antiquarian opinion'. (See Fig. 8) This was certainly still the case in the late fifteenth century, especially since, for

Fig. 8. Title page of Richard Grafton's *A Chronicle at large* (1569) illustrating the eclectic view of history still current in the latter half of the sixteenth century: with the Hebrews, Moses, Saul, David and Solomon balanced by their supposedly contemporaneous British rulers, Brute and his sons Locrine, Albanact and Camber. In the bottom centre sits Elizabeth I enthroned, flanked by William the Conqueror and Henry VIII.

a time, these historical myths seemed to be especially relevant to Henry Tudor's conflict with Richard III.

Naturally, the most fervent expressions of enthusiasm for the Tudor cause occurred in Wales, where there was a deliberate attempt by the bards to foster support for Henry against Richard III who had forfeited the loyalty of the Welsh Yorkists by the extinction of the line of Edward IV (Jones 1917–18). In the spate of vaticinatory verse predicting the Tudor triumph, references to the *British History* abound. Brutus, Cadwalader, the dragon prophecy and every other likely symbol are pressed into service in the outburst spawned by the impending struggle between Henry and Richard. But this was no novelty. Henry Tudor was merely the last of a long line of Welsh messiahs whose success had been prophesied by the bards, generally with unsatisfactory results, throughout the fifteenth century. These poets were not concerned with the English dynastic struggles but were seeking a great Welsh leader whose like had not been seen since the days of Owen Glendower and, accordingly, they vaunted a succession of heroes: Griffith ap Nicholas, Jasper Tudor, William Herbert and, finally, Henry of Richmond, Jasper Tudor's nephew. Moreover, the Tudors were not the first royal line to have a Welsh descent suitable for bardic exploitation. The Yorkists themselves had a valid genealogy which was celebrated, for example, by Lewis Glyn Cothi, later a fervent apologist for Henry Tudor but who had once hailed Edward IV as a descendant of Gwladys Duy, daughter of Llewellyn the Great, and had appealed to the King, as a *royal Welshman*, to rid the land of oppression. Similarly, Gutto'r Glyn had asserted the British origin of Edward IV and had asked him to descend upon the 'deceits and wrongs of Wales' (Evans 1915: chapter 1). Many poets offered their panegyrics first to one party and then the other but they were all consistent in their nationalism and sincere in their support of both Edward IV and Henry Tudor. It is, therefore, clear that we should not make too much of these eulogies of Henry as evidence of a new cult. They were part of a long tradition, and probably owe their large-scale survival to the fact that, unlike other candidates for Welsh support, Henry Tudor not only gained the throne but also succeeded in establishing a dynasty.

This question of the survival of evidence is especially suggestive when we turn to the more formal and systematic statements on lineage in contemporary genealogies. The occasional appearance of Brutus or Cadwalader in Tudor manuscript pedigrees has sometimes been cited as proof that Henry VII and his successors consciously manipulated the *British History* for propagandist purposes. However, earlier during the fifteenth century there had been a proliferation of elaborate genealogies, usually in the form of rolls, seeking to trace the kings of England back to very remote forebears. This may have been due to the political

uncertainties engendered by the rivalry of Henry VI, Richard Duke of
York and Edward IV; but it may also be regarded as part of a much
wider, intuitive quest for historical and emotional stability, which developed as the feudal bases of society became increasingly remote and
ineffective. Whatever the cause, it is striking that, during the reign of
Henry VI, production of such genealogies greatly increased: though
few of these are especially interesting apart from one illuminated page
showing the descendants of St Louis in the form of a fleur-de-lis.
Here the central branch gives the direct line of French kings to
Charles IV; the left hand the Valois line to Charles VI and Catherine;
the right hand the English kings from Edward I; and all three unite in
Henry VI (British Library MS. Royal 15.E.vi). Several of these genealogies include a conventional summary of the *British History*, though
they always indicate a complete break with the coming of the Saxons
and, indeed, often have a line ruled right across the roll before the
Saxon heptarchy begins. Sometimes the British line does stagger on
for a while, parallel to the English, before it peters out at about the
time of Edward I or Edward II. But it never has any connection with
the central royal line leading to Henry VI, simply because there was no
such connection to be made (Anglo 1961: 21, 41−3).

It was, however, a different matter with Edward IV. His father
Richard, Duke of York, was the son of Anne, daughter of Roger
Mortimer, Earl of March. And the Mortimers could trace *their* descent
to the marriage, in 1230, between Ralph de Mortimer and Gwladys
Duy, daughter of Llewellyn ap Iorwoeth. This in turn led back to
Rhodri Mawr who died in 878 and whose descent was traced, by
medieval authorities, to the famous Cadwalader, the last British king.
The Mortimer family had itself dwelt on this claim to antiquity, and
the Wigmore Manuscript, dating from the late fourteenth century,
includes a genealogy tracing the family's descent back to Gwladys Duy
and thence to Brutus the Trojan (Giffin 1941: 109−20). This Yorkist
lineage was generally acknowledged by genealogists and it is even
included in *Wriothesley's Book*, a Tudor collection of armorials which,
since it also gives Henry VIII's descent from Cadwalader, must be
considered impartial (British Library MS. Additional 46,354,
fols.59−61).

With only a few exceptions, Edward IV's own genealogies indicate
this descent and emphasize his relationship with the early rulers of
Britain (Anglo 1961: 22−4). Several simply assume a knowledge of the
British History and commence at a much later period, while still stressing
the British origin of the Mortimers. One roll, for example, begins its
line *Britannia* with Roger Mortimer, and includes a second genealogy
with the Welsh line showing the marriage of Gwladys Duy and continuing to Edward IV, 'kyng of more brutteyn and of ffrance'. Another

roll begins its British line with Llewellyn, Prince of Wales, 'heres cadwaladri', and leads — via the Mortimers — to Richard, Duke of York, heir to Britain, France and Spain, and finally to Edward IV, indubitable king of those realms. This manuscript also includes extracts from Gildas, Bede and Geoffrey of Monmouth; and, by repeating the story of the angel's revelation to Cadwalader, implies that Edward IV is the fulfiller of the prophecy. The same idea is suggested in another genealogy which begins its British line with Iorwoeth, Prince of North Wales and 'verus heres Cadwalladro qui vocatur Rubeus Draco', gives the prophecy to Cadwalader, and traces the British line through the Mortimers to Edward IV. Edward's role as the prince who fulfils British destiny is even more strongly suggested in a genealogy which begins its British line with Gwladys Duy daughter of Llewellyn, heir to Brutus, continues to Edward IV, and concludes with the angel's prophecy.

Sometimes Edward's pedigree is traced right back to Adam: though, even on these occasions, the crucial line is through the Trojans. One such genealogy gives a Latin digest of the *British History*, followed by an English summary illustrated with coloured arms showing the King with the triple crown of Britain, France and Spain upon his head. Similar in scope is a roll chronicle illustrating the descent of Richard, Duke of York, 'Ryght eyre of Brute fraunce and spayne', and Edward IV from Camber, son of Brutus. But the most striking document relating to Edward's British ancestry is an elaborate roll chronicle in which each name in the British line, starting with Caduanus, is accompanied by the rubrics *Brutus*, *Rubius* and *Draco*; while the English line, stemming from the Saxon kings, is significantly accompanied by the rubrics *Albus* and *Draco*. The roll reaches its climax with the rivalry between Henry VI who, as the culmination of the English line, is the *Albus Draco*, and Edward IV who concludes the story as the triumphant British *Rubius Draco*. The moral is stressed by a conclusion summarizing the *British History*. With the coming of Brutus the land had been called the *Rede Dragon* or else *Brutane*. In Cadwalader's time, the British had been expelled for their sins and, according to an angelic prophecy, would not again inherit the land until the Saxon invaders had sinned in the same way. The name of the returning conqueror would be *Rubius Draco* and he would be the true heir to England, Scotland and Wales, since the three kingdoms had originally been one. This is the clearest possible exposition of the idea that Edward IV was the returning hero of the Trojan line. He was the British messiah. He was the Red Dragon (British Library MS. Additional 18,268.A).

But who cared? Certainly many Welsh patriots did: but these manuscript genealogies were designed for an English, not a Celtic, market; and it is difficult now to be clear as to their purpose. Their survival in such numbers, together with the fact that some of them are handsomely-executed presentation copies, has suggested that they were a form of 'propaganda' aimed not, of course, at a mass audience, but at an educated élite consisting of the 'nobility and gentry, and the increasingly educated commercial classes' (Allen 1979: 189). That they were designed for an élite is undeniable: but propaganda has, by definition, to propagate and persuade and it is wholly unlikely that the allegiance of any fifteenth-century intellectual — whether magnate, gentleman or merchant — would have been swayed by a family tree demonstrating a link between Yorkists and Trojans. It is more likely that such genealogies appealed only to people already committed politically; and that the tracing of an ancient royal lineage, highly spiced with prophecies, would have afforded a pleasure scarcely different from modern indulgence in the craze for pedigree-hunting.

If modern theories about Tudor interest in the *British History* were well founded, we would expect to find it expressed in a paper antiquity similar to that of Edward IV. Yet, in fact, the reign of Henry VII produced few examples of this genre. The nearest approach to an official statement of Henry Tudor's British origin is in Bernardus Andreas's *Historia* which begins with an account of the King's royal descent — from Cadwalader on his father's side, and from John of Gaunt on his mother's — and states that the ancient prophecy to Cadwalader has been fulfilled in the person of Henry VII (Gairdner 1858: 9–11). Bernardus Andreas was Henry's historiographer and poet laureate and — though he was singularly undistinguished in both capacities, and though his history is scrappy, incomplete and jejune — his inclusion of this British material makes it at least possible that there may have been some interest on the King's part. And this view, superficially at least, seems to be corroborated by the account, in David Powel's edition of Lhoyd's *Historie of Cambria*, of a commission appointed by Henry VII to examine the pedigree of Owen Tudor. Indeed, according to Powel, the return of that commission was still extant at the time of publication in 1584:

There was a commission at this time [*c.* 1490] directed from king Henrie the seaventh, to the Abbot of Llan Egwest, Doctor Owen Poole, chanon of Hereford, and Iohn King, harold, to make inquisition concerning the parentage of the said Owen, who comming to Wales, trauelled in that matter, and used the helps of Sir Iohn Leyaf, Guttyn Owen Bardh, Grufffyth ap Lhewelyn ap Euan Vachan, and others in the search of the Brytish or Welsh bookes of petigrees out of the which they drew his perfect genelogie from the ancient kings of Brytaine and the Princes of

Wales, and so returned their commission: which returne is extant at this date to be seene.

(Lhoyd 1584: 391)

A manuscript in the Royal collection (18.A.1xxv), dating from the reign of Edward VI, sets forth Henry VII's descent, by various lines, from the Welsh princes and British kings and itself claims to agree with the best chronicles in Wales: 'and was at the true examinacion off the same the abbat of Llynegwestill, maister doctour Even Pole, syr Johan Lyaff, prist, Guttyn Owen, Robert ap Hoell ap Thomas, Johan Kyng, Madoc ap Llywelyn ap Hoell and Gruffith ap Llywelyn Vichan, which hathe founde and proved this good and true lynaige'. This list corresponds to the one provided by Powel (the two extra names being, presumably, the 'others' whom he mentions) and must refer to the same examination. Moreover, the facts that Owen Pole, Canon of Hereford, died in 1509, and that Guttyn Owen was one of the most famous Welsh bards of the late fifteenth century, indicate that the manuscript is a copy of a document dating from the reign of Henry VII. It belonged to Humphrey Lhoyd whose name appears on the first folio. Lhoyd's manuscript history of Wales was completed in 1559 and was the basis for Powel's edition but, since it ends at the year 1294, the later chapter, in the first printed edition, must have been written by Powel who made considerable use of the manuscripts collected by Lhoyd and altered the originals to suit his own purposes. The Royal manuscript, therefore, is almost certainly the very document referred to by Powel as being extant in 1584. But it contains nothing to suggest that it was the work of a royally-appointed commission, and it seems that Powel was dressing up the evidence to make it more impressive.

Apart from this dubious story, there is little evidence in Henry VII's reign of official interest in the British pedigree (Anglo 1961: 25−6, 46−7). One illuminated genealogy traces Henry's descent both from John of Gaunt and from the British kings; while a *Genealogia domini henrici Septimi regis anglorum a Cadwaladro* is included in a pedigree of English kings accompanying a Latin chronicle preserved among the Harleian Manuscripts. On the other hand there is striking evidence of a lack of concern about the Tudor British descent in a surviving roll pedigree of Prince Arthur. This shows Henry VII deriving from John of Gaunt through his mother and from Katharine, wife of Henry V, through his father. Yet not only is Owen Tudor *not* mentioned, but the Welsh line deriving from Cadwalader is shown leading via the Mortimers to Edward IV. Prince Arthur is here regarded as heir to the British heritage through his mother, Elizabeth of York, not through his father, Henry Tudor; and it is obvious that this lineage was regarded as insignificant in comparison with the English royal line.

Henry VIII was even less concerned than his father to proclaim British ancestry. Indeed, by his time, the fifteenth-century obsession with the king's lineage seems to have withered away (Anglo 1961: 26–7, 47–8). Royal roll pedigrees become scarce and none of them depict Henry VIII's British origins. One roll, starting with Adam, includes the British kings but does not connect them with the later English line culminating in Henry VIII; another begins with Edward I; while a third only opens its account with the Saxon Egbert and Rollo, the Norman. The most ambitious of these genealogies also begins with Egbert and includes the Norman and Angevin lines. It was intended, by its compiler, not as a repetition of unproven myths and medieval accretions but as a serious attempt to analyse the political history bearing upon the English royal house. He declares his lofty purpose from the outset:

> The manyfould errors dayly used amongis such as Imprint bookes making diuerse abstractis, with abrigid historyis lardyng their workis with diuers new inuentions to thintent that such may haue gaynes and seke nogt the secrete of the cronicles that is to say the lyniall descentes, maryages, and affinities with combinacions of yeris, wherfore in excluding all such abusions here folowing you shall see the veritie and originall accorde of diuerse descentes. That is to say how the duches of normandy, of Gascoine and guyen, aniow, maigne, turayne, pontw, tholose and france haue byne annexid to the Crowne of Englind wyth dyuers other duchiese and counteis of Englond in lyke maner joynid. By the which you may perceive clerely theffect Begynnyng at the yeres of our lord viii^c and xl and so contynwid unto the raigne of our souerayne Lord King Henry the viij^t.
>
> (British Library MS. Lansdowne Rolls 6)

In this elaborate survey, Henry VII appears as the son of Margaret, daughter of John Beaufort, and Edmund, Earl of Richmond: but it is significant that Edmund's descent is not shown; and his Welsh forebears are absent. The document – which goes on to detail the early career of Henry VIII whose victory at Flodden in 1513 is the last information given – is carefully written and researched; and it suggests a new critical attitude to history. Later, in the middle of the sixteenth century, there certainly was an academic debate over the status of the *British History* which continued to find passionate defenders of whom perhaps the most notable was the antiquary, John Leland. In general, however, educated opinion was on the side of his adversaries; and such scepticism is reflected in the jettisoning of the old myths in this genealogical roll.

Scepticism and a critical approach to history rarely characterized civic pageantry, and they were certainly not in evidence during Henry VII's first progress. The King was still fresh from the Continent and the idea that he represented the return of the original British dynasty was in the air. At York, Henry was greeted as a lineal descendant by the mighty warrior, King Ebrancus who was, according to Geoffrey of Monmouth, founder of the city and a contemporary of King David and Silvius Latinus; while at Worcester, as we have seen, it had been intended to greet Henry as fulfiller of the prophecy made to Cadwalader. Nevertheless, subsequent pageant series do not insist upon this motif and there was never again any reference as specific as the projected speech at Worcester. In the London pageants for Prince Arthur's marriage in 1501, there is no allusion to the British descent, and the pedigree emphasized was the line from John of Gaunt, who was the ancestor common to both Arthur and his bride, Katharine of Aragon.

In 1522, when Henry VIII and the Emperor Charles V made their entry into London, it was again the descent from John of Gaunt, appropriate to both rulers, which was featured, along with a genealogical tree showing their joint descent from Alphonso the Wise of Castile. Neither the London pageants for Anne Boleyn in 1533, Edward VI in 1547, nor Mary in 1553 displayed any Tudor genealogies; but the joint entry of Philip and Mary into London in 1554 included a genealogical tree taking root from an old man lying on his left side, 'with a long white beard and close croune on his heade, and a sceptour in his ryght hand, and a ball imperial in his lefte; which olde man signified Edward the third, of whom both their majesties are lineally descended' (see Fig. 9). Finally, when Elizabeth I entered London in 1559, the first pageant to greet her was 'The vniting of the two houses of Lancastre and Yorke', which took the Queen's descent no further back than the marriage of Henry VII and Elizabeth of York. Presumably, by that time, this was far enough to satisfy anybody.[41]

The evidence of civic pageantry, like that of the genealogical rolls, suggests that early interest in the British descent of the Tudors soon declined. And this view can be corroborated by pursuing the fortunes of King Arthur. Arthurianism remains the most popular aspect of modern attitudes toward royal 'propaganda', especially during the reigns of the early Tudors. It has been maintained that King Arthur, the central figure in the *British History*, became equally central in an efflorescence of historical primitivism as the new dynasty sought to establish an antiquity rivalling that of the continental monarchies.[42] The foundation for this idea is the choice of Winchester as the birthplace for Henry VII's first son and the fact that he was christened *Arthur*.

Genealogically speaking there could be no connection – even in fifteenth-century terms – between the Tudors and King Arthur, whose line, whenever indicated on roll pedigrees, always ends amid the civil

Fig. 9. Title page of John Stow's *The Annales of England* (1592) showing the roses of York and Lancaster growing from the recumbent figure of Edward III. This theme appears in the London pageants of 1554.

wars which recalled him from the Continent. On the other hand, propaganda generally depends for its effect on evocation rather than precision, and there is no denying the Arthurian resonances of Winchester which was particularly noted, during the fifteenth century, as the home of the round table preserved in the Great Hall (Hardyng, ed. Ellis 1812: 146). Moreover, according to Edward Hall, the very name *Arthur* had been a potent symbol: 'Englishmen no-more reioysed then outwarde nacions and foreyne prynces trymbled and quaked, so much was that name to all nacions terrible and formidable' (Hall, ed. Ellis 1809: 428). Certainly, Henry VII must have had greater confidence in the name than Edward IV, who merely bestowed it upon one of his bastards, Arthur Plantagenet, later Viscount Lisle. Even Francis Bacon, casting the eye of a historian over the whole affair, wrote that Henry VII chose the name 'Arthur' to honour the British race from which he himself derived, 'according to the name of that ancient worthy King of the Britons, in whose acts there is truth enough to make him famous, besides that which is fabulous' (Bacon, ed. Spedding 1858: 43–4).

Prince Arthur's birth encouraged a burst of enthusiasm amongst the continental poetasters of the court circle, who wrote as though it heralded a return of the Golden Age of peace – very much in the fashion of Vergil's fourth *Eclogue*. The latter motif had already achieved a considerable vogue in Italian political verse but was new to England when Pietro Carmeliano, a Brescian sycophant, who had only shortly before praised Richard III as a model ruler, made it the crowning point of a poem celebrating the end of civil strife in England. This tells of Henry VII's return from exile, his success at Bosworth Field, the death of Richard III (now metamorphosed into a bloody tyrant), and the marriage with Elizabeth, heiress to the house of York. It ends with the fruit of the union – that is the birth of a prince who will secure the future and make certain that England will never again fall into civil discord. A new age of peace is at hand and the great King Arthur, buried for so many centuries, now returns as prophesied: though this prophecy, it should be noted, was not part of the original *British History*. Similar sentiments were expressed by Giovanni de'Giglis, papal collector in England, who wrote that, after so many centuries, the great days of King Arthur had returned; and by Bernardus Andreas who professed to see, beneath the form of the new prince, the image of the first Arthur (Anglo 1961: 29–30). This tiny cluster of courtly eulogists, heralding the advent of a new Golden Age, is not without interest. But their conventional expressions of joy, naturally evoked by the consolidation of the new dynasty, do not constitute evidence either for an enduring cult of King Arthur or for a propaganda campaign. Their work was intended for the King: and, while he may well have enjoyed the praise, he hardly needed to be informed about his own motives or persuaded as to the rectitude of his procedures.

Obviously the combination of Winchester and the name *Arthur* in 1486 was not fortuitous. It must have been suggested by their prominence in the *British History*: but the theme was not developed and there was certainly nothing as systematic as that 'cult of King Arthur' discerned by some modern scholars. It has, for example, been suggested that the

main events of Prince Arthur's short life were celebrated in verse and
pageantry reflecting the glory of his namesake (Millican 1932: 16–24;
Kendrick 1950: 36). Yet this was not the case. When the Prince visited
Coventry in 1498, it is true that he was welcomed by a pageant of the
Nine Worthies whose spokesman was King Arthur: but this is not the
whole story, and two qualifications are necessary. First, the point of his
speech was not genealogical but was simply intended to draw attention
to the name parallel, which was a favoured technique in fifteenth-
century Coventry pageantry. The second and much more important
qualification is methodological. To isolate one character – when there
were two further pageants in the series, with speeches by Dame
Fortune and Saint George, neither of whom makes any allusion to
King Arthur or to the *British History* – is a trick that may be used to
establish the primacy of almost any image. The Coventry pageants
were not primarily concerned with either King Arthur or the *British
History*; and even if they had been, the spectacle was politically insignificant and intellectually meagre (Harris 1907–13: II, 589–90).

By far the most elaborate spectacles associated with Prince Arthur
were those organized to mark his marriage with Katharine of Aragon in
November 1501. The successful negotiation of this match was a triumph
of early Tudor diplomacy and was, accordingly, celebrated at court by
the costliest entertainments of the reign, and by the City of London
with a pageant series which was to remain the most intellectually
complex of the entire Tudor period. If King Arthur ever were the
object of a Tudor 'cult', then these wedding festivities should have
been the occasion to display it; and it has, in fact, been claimed that
the civic pageants comprised a 'compliment to the Welsh ancestry of
the reigning house' (Greenlaw 1932: 180). The truth of the matter is
that there is only one allusion to King Arthur in the entire series and
this concerns the astrological and astronomical theme, (suggested by
the parallel *Arthur* and *Arcturus*), around which the pageants were built.
As for the entertainments at court: there was nothing in them relating
to the *British History* or King Arthur.[43]

Recently, there has been an ingenious attempt to establish an Arthurian
leitmotiv linking the disguisings at court with a pageant, depicting the
kings of France, England and Spain, prepared by the King's Council
to greet Arthur and Katharine at the West door of St Paul's after their
marriage. On the basis of a single reference in *The Great Chronicle
of London*, which states that the 'middylmest' figure in the pageant
'Representid kyng arthur' (Thomas and Thornley 1938: 310), it has
been argued that the scene depicted Arthur receiving the homage of
Charlemagne and some 'royal Spanish worthy' (Kipling 1977: 97). Yet
none of this is suggested either in the chronicle or in the much fuller
description written by a herald. The latter does not mention Arthur;

and he makes it clear that the King of France, with his red roses, white greyhound and white hart, is a Lancastrian prince — not Charlemagne. Nobody is doing obeisance to anybody. And the King of England, with his red roses and red dragon — 'beying in the mydds of a shypp, and appiered above the seid shypp by the myddill' — is a pageantic interpretation of the image of the upper half of a king emerging from a ship, which had decorated the obverse of some of the most important English gold coins since the reign of Edward III up to and including Henry VII's ryall, and beyond (see Fig. 10). If this king of England represented anybody, it was Henry Tudor himself.

Just over four months later Prince Arthur was dead and whatever Arthurianism there may have been at the early Tudor court was interred with him. His brother, Henry, who succeeded him as Prince of Wales, came to the throne in 1509 and the early years of his reign witnessed an unprecedented flurry of tournaments, disguisings and masks: but it was not until July 1520 that King Arthur reappeared in a court festival. This was as a statue, holding a round table, set up over the gateway to the vestibule of a temporary theatre built by Henry VIII at Calais for the entertainment of the Emperor Charles V. There was no attempt on this occasion to give Arthur any specifically Tudor significance; the poem inscribed beneath the statue is a general exhortation to both princes to rule with honour and to follow chivalric ideals; and the rest of the theatre's imagery makes it clear that Arthur is intended here to represent not Britain but rather the international brotherhood of chivalry of which Henry VIII and Charles V were shining examples. This Anglo-Imperial meeting followed immediately after the more renowned Anglo-French interview at the Field of Cloth of Gold where, contrary to general belief, there was no Arthurian symbolism whatever. The last Henrician appearance of King Arthur was in one of the nine pageants prepared for the joint entry of Henry VIII and Charles V into London in 1522 when the British king was represented, seated at the round table, attended by subject kings. The difficulty about this example is that, in the explicatory speech delivered by a child, it is the Emperor (not Henry) who is compared to the great Arthur (Anglo 1961: 33–4).

Apart from an appearance among the Nine Worthies for the entry of Philip and Mary in 1554, King Arthur does not figure in any other English pageant series during the sixteenth century. Nor did he ever occupy that dominant place in court entertainments which has sometimes been assigned to him. He did, however, loom large in the antiquarian controversy over the *British History*, and in this respect it is interesting to note that John Rastell — lawyer, printer, playwright and revels artist intimately connected with both court festivals and civic pageantry — was very critical of the whole corpus of Galfridian material. In the

Fig. 10. Ryal coins: Henry VII, Henry VIII, Mary, Elizabeth I (Hocking nos.789, 814, 928, 947).

prologue to his hisorical survey, *Pastyme of People*, Rastell discusses the authenticity of the *British History* and, within a couple of pages, is able to pull the whole absurd fabric to pieces: though he concludes that, since these stories may yet serve as valuable exemplars of good and evil, he will not excise them from his history. Similarly, in the main body of his work, Rastell states that he will neither deny nor affirm the story of Arthur but will 'let every man be at his lyberte to beleue ther in what he lyste'. Yet, by the time he offers this concession, he has already drawn attention to the fact that neither Bede nor other con- temporaries ever mention Arthur; and has consistently qualified his references to the British king's extraordinary and unlikely achievements with a standard refrain indicating dubiety – 'as Galfridus wrytyth'. Most striking of all is the devastating 'some men thynk' technique, soon to be made famous by Christopher Saint German but here used by Rastell to marshal arguments against the authenticity of Arthur's seal, preserved at Westminster (Rastell, ed. Dibdin 1811: 3–8, 106–7).

Pastyme of People was published in 1529, and it is ironic that, less than two years after Rastell's bold display of historical scepticism, King Arthur's spurious achievements should have made their closest approach to the central issues of Henrician politics. In January 1531, Chapuys, the Imperial ambassador, reported at great length to Charles V upon a bizarre interview he had just enjoyed with the Duke of Norfolk, Stephen Gardiner, and the Treasurer (Bergenroth *et al.* 1862–1954: IV.i, no.598). The Duke had been arguing that the popes of old had vainly attempted to usurp authority in England and that Henry VIII's predecessors had never consented to it. Furthermore, the Duke continued, kings were· before popes; the King of England was absolute master in his own kingdom, acknowledging no superior; that an Englishman, Brennus, had once reduced Rome under his obedience; that Constantius had reigned in England; and that Helen, the mother of Constantius, was English by birth. There were several other similar observations which, as Chapuys laconically observed, were as 'little pertinent to the matter in question as the above'. Then King Arthur was dragged into the fray. Apparently, the Duke had very recently shown the French ambassador a copy of the inscription on the tomb of King Arthur: though Chapuys affects not to have understood 'to which of the Arthurs he alluded'! Then the Duke produced from his pouch a parchment roll with the inscription in large letters especially transcribed for Chapuys: *PATRICIUS ARCTURUS BRITANNIE, GALLIE, GERMANIE, DACIE IMPERATOR*. Chapuys's reply was masterly:

> My answer was that I was sorry to see that he was not entitled also Emperor of Asia, *IMPERATOR ASIE*, as he might have left

the present king Henry for his successor in such vast dominions; but as all things in this world were so subject to change, it was reasonable that an English monarch of our days should conquer a portion of the provinces above named, since in those very countries men had been found who had conquered and held for a long time this very kingdom of England, where the succession of William of Normandy still lasted. If by shewing me the inscription the Duke meant that the present King Henry might be such a conqueror as king Arthur, I could not help observing that the Assyrians, Persians, Macedonians, and Romans had also made great conquests, and everyone knew what had become of their empire.

Obviously all this nonsense had been intended, by Norfolk, to impress Chapuys with Henry VIII's imperial status. It failed lamentably. Such arguments were too easily punctured by a few sharp thrusts of common sense; and possibly somebody in authority appreciated this vulnerability. When, in the preamble to the Act in Restraint of Appeals to Rome of April 1533, there is the oft-quoted exordium, 'Where by divers sundry old authentic histories and chronicles it is manifestly declared and expressed that this realm of England is an empire, and so hath been accepted in the world', the deliberately vague reference must be to the whole panoply of historical sources which had been scoured for the King by a team of scholars and submitted to him in the manuscript known as the *Collectanea satis copiosa*. These certainly included Geoffrey of Monmouth but embraced much else besides (Guy 1986: 156–63). The breach with Rome and the augmentation of regal power were matters far too serious to depend merely upon the risky and suspect myths of the *British History*.

Just as, among those myths, Arthur was the most famous figure, so the red dragon was the most famous symbol. Its fundamental source, as for the vast Arthurian edifice erected by Geoffrey of Monmouth and his followers, is the ninth-century *Historia Brittonum* of Nennius which tells of a vision, conjured up by Merlin, of two rival dragons symbolizing the struggle between Saxons and Britons and of the ultimate triumph of the latter. This dragon prophecy, with its Galfridian embellishments, became one of the best-known historical ideas of the Middle Ages. It was used in the *Rubius Draco* genealogy of Edward IV and it was also closely associated with Henry VII and his successors. However, with the Tudors, it underwent a curious and very important metamorphosis (Anglo 1961: 37–40).

The appearance of the red dragon at the end of the fifteenth century is usually interpreted as an allusion to the Tudor Welsh descent which was traced to Cadwalader, the last British king; and the creature is customarily referred to as the *Red Dragon of Cadwalader* or the *Welsh*

Dragon. Yet the compilers of books of arms in the fifteenth century never assigned the badge to Cadwalader whose arms were invariably given as azure, a cross *patté fitché or*. The first occasion when a dragon is associated unequivocally with Cadwalader seems to be in a sixteenth-century book of banners and badges, where *Le Roy Cadwalader* is represented by his customary arms supported by a dragon, or and gules, with wings expanded. This combination probably reflects confusion between Cadwalader, the prophecy made to him, and the original dragon prophecy, and it is, in any case, an isolated instance. The weight of armorial evidence is against a Cadwaladrian dragon. Further evidence − negative yet cogent − is afforded by contemporary chroniclers who write of the beast as the *Red Dragon Dreadful* but never connect it with the name *Cadwalader*.

Contemporary accounts and later descriptions of Henry VII's presentation of his battle standards at St Paul's in 1485 do not refer to his dragon standard as being *of Cadwalader*; while the *Empcions* for his coronation, in addition to providing for red dragon embroidery, also provide for a 'Trappour of Cad Walladeres armes' − implying that the two were habitually thought of as separate items. In addition to all this, the general history of the dragon badge casts doubt not only on its association with Cadwalader but also on its special relationship to Wales. The ensign had been used by the Romans, the Saxons and the royal house of England. The dragon banner had been unfurled for Richard I, John, Henry III and Edward III; and there is no reason to suppose that Wales enjoyed a monopoly of dragons or, indeed, that the Welsh princes had made much play with the symbol prior to the fifteenth century (Tatlock 1933: 223−35).

Of course, none of this invalidates the importance attached to the dragon prophecy in armorial and political ideology after Geoffrey's *Historia Regum Britanniae*. The red dragon became an acknowledged symbol of the *British History*, especially the return of British dominion over the Saxons. It was used in this way when Edward IV was shown both as *Rubius Draco* and as fulfiller of the prophecy made to Cadwalader − confusion between the two prophecies already being apparent. A similar concurrence of British descent and dragon badge may be seen in the career of Owen Glendower, who traced his lineage back to Camber, son of Brutus. On the field of battle, Owen used a dragon standard; and his Great Seal showed him mounted, both he and his horse being crested with a winged dragon or wyvern. That these were indirect allusions to his British ancestry is likely: but their immediate sources were more specific than the generalized British dragon imagery. In Geoffrey's *Historia*, Utherpendragon was encouraged, after the appearance of a dragon-like star favourably interpreted by Merlin, to have two golden dragon ensigns made, one for the

The Standerd
of the Dragon
borne by Sr George
Bourchier

The Horse ledd by two Querries

Fig. 11. Standard of the Dragon from the funeral procession of Elizabeth I. British Library MS. Additional 35,324, fol.28ʳ.

church at Winchester, the other to be carried into battle. Subsequently, Uther's son, Arthur, is reported to have used a *vexillum aureus draco* in his Roman campaign, and he is also described as having worn a helmet *simulacro draconis*. These standards and crests were the prototypes for Owen Glendower's seal and battle ensign, and they have nothing to do with Cadwalader and little to do with the dragon prophecy in its original form.

Jasper Tudor also made use of the dragon badge, and it has been suggested that he was influenced by the fact that Owen Glendower was cousin to his father, Owen Tudor (Tatlock 1933: 232). But again this is a unilinear approach to the history of the symbol. Jasper, like Glendower, claimed a British descent. He was also a potential Welsh saviour and was hailed as the fulfiller of Merlin's prophecy — one who would gain the 'victory of the red dragon over the dishonoured white' (Evans 1915: 8). Jasper's dragon derived, not directly from Glendower's, but from a common and more distant source.

Like his uncle Jasper, Henry VII consciously acknowledged the dragon symbol, but never more strikingly than at the beginning of his

reign. When he made his entry into London after Bosworth he presented at St Paul's three standards which, presumably, he had borne into battle — 'oon was of the Armys of Seynt George. The secund a Red ffyry dragon peyntid upon whyte and Grene Sarcenet, and the third was a Baner of Tarteron bett wyth a dun Cowe' — allusions respectively to the realm of England and to the British and Beaufort connections (Thomas and Thornley 1938: 238—9). Again, at the ceremony of creating knights of the Bath prior to his coronation, Henry instituted a new pursuivant whom he named *Rougedragon* (Anglo 1960: 5). These instances — highlighted by the earlier identification of Edward IV with the same symbol — must be regarded as relevant to Henry Tudor's British ancestry as distinct from his specific descent from Cadwalader. They are in a tradition similar to the dragons of Owen Glendower and Jasper Tudor but not necessarily derived from them.

The later history of the dragon shows little development: or, more precisely, it shows how symbols can speedily become detached from their original meaning. The dragon rarely served as a theme in literature, music or pageant; and its greatest prominence was as an heraldic supporter. As a moulded figure it featured with the other royal beasts and badges among the ornamentation of the London pageant series of 1501, and in pictures of Tudor pavilions and temporary palaces such as that for the Field of Cloth of Gold, now at Hampton Court.

Similarly, it is to be seen on the roof bosses at St George's Chapel Windsor, among the Hampton Court beasts, and amid the display of Tudor beasts and badges at King's College Chapel, Cambridge. It is drawn in manuscripts, woven into tapestries and embossed on gold plate. In short, it became a decorative commonplace so that, as the dragon was absorbed into the menagerie of royal beasts, its original British signification dwindled. It became one of the best known of all heraldic animals: but it symbolized the Tudor dynasty rather than the Tudor descent (see Fig. 11).

Chapter Three

HENRY VI: THE LANCASTRIAN SAINT

Welcome Nevew, welcome my Cousyn dere,
Next of my Blood descended by Alyaunce,
Chosen by Grace of God both fer and ner,
To be myn Heir in Englande and in Fraunce,
Ireland, Wales, with al the Apertenaunce
Of the hole Tytle which I sumtyme had,
All is thyn owne, wherefor I am right glad.

I am Henry the VIth. sobre and sad,
Thy great Uncle, sumtyme of England King.
Full XXXIX Yeres this Realme myself I had,
And of the People had the Governyng.
Slaine was I, Martir by great Tormenting,
In Chartesey buried, translate unto Windesore,
Ther logge I now, and arst ther was I bore.

(Leland 1770: IV, 192)

Just as the speech of *Janitor*, from the pageant series prepared for
Henry VII at Worcester in 1486, served to introduce the theme of the
British History, so the above verses — from the same abortive show —
introduce another dynastic issue. They are from a long speech which
was to have been delivered by a figure representing Henry VI; and they
summarize some of the principal ideas, concerning that unfortunate
monarch, which remained current throughout the reign of Henry VII.
The figure of the dead king refers to the blood relationship between
himself and the first Tudor, and stresses his own regal authority. Then
he says that he was foully murdered and died a martyr. And finally he
mentions that he had been buried first at Chertsey before his translation
to Windsor.

Henry VI had proved an embarrassment to the Yorkist party almost
from the moment of his murder, and they had been forced to face up
to the unpleasant rumours circulating about the manner of his death.
One apologist wrote that Henry VI had been in the Tower when he

received news of the utter defeat of his party, and realized the hopeless-
ness of recovery. He took the news, wrote the chronicler, 'to so great
dispite, ire and indingnation, that, of pure displeasure, and melencoly,
he dyed'. But in the margin of the manuscript there has been added,
after 'dyed', the phrase 'or was mordered', thereby indicating the
doubts and fears which shrouded the melancholy end of the inept and
unlucky monarch (Bruce 1838: 38, 46). The Milanese ambassador in
France, however, was in no doubt about the matter and wrote to
Galeazzo Maria Sforza that Edward IV, seeing that the Prince Edward
and other Lancastrian leaders had been killed, chose to complete the
work and had caused Henry VI to be murdered in the Tower. Rumour
had it, continued the Italian, that Henry's queen had also been put to
death. Edward had, in short, chosen to crush the seed (Hinds, ed.
1912: no. 220).

It was not long before the Lancastrian king became the subject of
popular veneration and worship. He had been buried at Chertsey
Abbey, presumably because it was deemed to be an undistinguished
and insignificant place of sepulture — but not, it would seem, sufficiently
obscure to prevent a prompt outbreak of miracles. Moreover, as early
as 1473, an effigy of the dead king had somehow appeared on the choir
screen at York Minster, and within six years the matter had become so
serious that it was necessary for the Archbishop of York, Laurence
Booth, to take steps to suppress what was rapidly developing into a cult
of Henry VI. The Archbishop issued a strict injunction that no one was
to hold in veneration the statue or image of Henry, lately King of
England '*de facto et non de iure*'. The statue, he continued, was in
contempt of the Universal Church, an insult or contemnation of King
Edward IV, and a pernicious example to devout Christians. The veneration had to cease under pain of the law and punishment (Grosjean
1935: 157–8).[44]

The outcome of this official attack is not known: but the image was
still at York in 1516, which suggests that the cult had endured despite
Yorkist opposition. Moreover, while all this was going on, the Chertsey
miracles persisted to such an extent that, in 1484, Richard III had
Henry's body removed to Windsor where it was interred with great
ceremony. It was probably hoped that, by giving the ill-used corpse a
decent burial in a place of honour, the burden of hatred and suspicion
that had fallen on Richard's shoulders might be alleviated.

This was not the first occasion that a great figure in English politics
had been brought to a violent end and had then haunted and persecuted
his oppressors with posthumous miracles and threats of sanctity. The
most spectacularly successful of these was, of course, Thomas Becket
who responded to murder with such a series of miracles and so
flourishing a cult that he was canonized within three years and forced

Henry II to do public penance at his shrine. Others were, in the long run, less successful. Simon de Montfort, for example, had been spoken of, by most contemporary chroniclers, as a martyr; and miracles were reported at his tomb and on the spot where his body had been mutilated by his enemies. Indeed, the matter became sufficiently serious for an article to be included in the *Dictum de Kenilworth*, asking that the Church should prevent Simon from being regarded as a saint and should put a stop to the publication abroad of the supposed miracles attributed to him (Bémont 1930: 256–7).

Another instance of posthumous thaumaturgy was Thomas, Earl of Lancaster, who had been executed in 1322 by the supporters of Edward II. His tomb in Pontefract rapidly became the scene for wondrous cures; while an effigy, erected in St Paul's, produced similar effects. Indeed, the dead Earl became so popular that the King had to write to the Bishop of London urging him to do something to end the cult. Despite this, there were even attempts, in the early years of Edward III's reign, to canonize the Earl; and Capgrave, in his *Chronicle of England*, reports that the canonization was confirmed – though this was not really the case.[45]

Edward II himself gained a posthumous revenge. His own grisly death soon led to argument as to whether or not he, like Thomas of Lancaster, was a suitable candidate for canonization. It was claimed that he, too, had wrought miracles: but Knighton, who wrote about all this, warned his readers that imprisonment and violent death make no man a martyr unless his life had been truly holy (Knighton, ed. Lumby 1889: 443–4). Pilgrims in search of a new restorative were less inclined to be choosey and they swarmed to the supposed martyr's shrine in the Abbey of St Peter at Gloucester. In fact, the flow of visitors quickly led to changes in the fabric of the house. Edward III, who had earlier tried to obtain canonization for Thomas of Lancaster, now came as a pilgrim with others of the royal family, and their generous gifts resulted in the architectural glories which grew up about the body of the murdered monarch. Nevertheless, the popular canonization never became official (Tout 1934: 180–2). Such a curious and ill-based cult could not endure, and it gradually faded away – supplanted by popular expectations of more up-to-date and modish miracle workers in much the same way that dietetic and pharmaceutical fads wax and wane in our own age of faith.

The posthumous fate of Henry VI was very similar to those of his popularly canonized predecessors, as were the principal ideas exploited by Tudor apologists in this affair. It was maintained that he had been brutally murdered and had died a martyr; that he had possessed the gift of prophecy and had foretold the success of Henry VII; and that he was a holy worker of miracles.

The story that he had been murdered was sedulously promulgated. 'Howe this prince dyed', wrote John Rastell, 'there be dyvers opinyons; but the most common tale was, that he was styccked with a dagger, by the hands of Rycharde, duke of Glocester' (Rastell, ed. Dibdin 1811: 285). The pageant Henry VI at Worcester in 1486 did not name his assassin, but none the less stressed that he had suffered no natural death. John Warkworth wrote that Henry VI had been put to death, 'beynge thanne at the Toure the Duke of Gloucetre, brothere to Kynge Edwarde, and many other'. The next day he was brought to St Paul's where his face was exposed to the gaze of the multitude; but already his sanctity was manifest for his corpse bled at St Paul's and later, having been moved to Blackfriars, 'he blede new and fresche' (Warkworth, ed. Halliwell 1839: 21). Bernardus Andreas is more explicit. He tells how Richard, that thirster after human blood − 'humani sanguinis sititor' − was sent by Edward IV to murder Henry, whose death precipitated great calamities (Gairdner 1858: 23). And so the tale was perpetuated. Peter Carmelianus, in his poem on the birth of Prince Arthur, makes Henry VI himself declare that he had been deprived of the kingdom by Edward IV and murdered by that butcher Richard, Duke of Gloucester, a man disposed to every crime and who even slaughtered the children whom his brother left in his care (British Library MS. Additional 33,736, fols.4ᵛ−5ʳ). Practically every chronicler described the murder of Henry VI. Some − like More, Fabyan, Polydore Vergil and Hall − phrased their accounts to imply that, while Richard's responsibility was not entirely certain, it was most likely that he had committed the crime. Others, including Grafton, had no doubts at all. And this certainty eventually prevailed when Shakespeare has Henry VI slain while in the middle of a prophetic utterance. 'I'll hear no more', snarls the monstrous Richard, 'die, prophet, in thy speech' (*Henry VI*, Pt.3, V.vi).

The relationship between sanctity and prophecy has always been intimate, and the attribution of prophetic powers was a common feature of hagiography. Edward the Confessor, Thomas Becket and Ailred of Rievaulx were all credited with such gifts; and Henry VI's alleged ability to foretell the future was similarly noted by Tudor apologists. For example, in Carmelianus's poem, Henry VI appears as spokesman for the convocation of saints in heaven, called together by God to find a remedy for the civil discord that had tormented England for so long. The saints had suggested to God that King Henry VI − already assigned a place amongst the heavenly élite − was best qualified to counsel on this problem; and there follows an *Oratio Divi henrici Sexti ad deum* in which the monarch advises that the only solution to England's calamities would be the union of the two warring houses of Lancaster and York. This desirable end could be accomplished by the marriage of Elizabeth, Edward IV's daughter who, through the extinction of the male heirs, inherited her father's rights, and Henry of Richmond who had taken refuge from Edward's sword in Brittany. The solution is heartily approved by God and is speedily put into effect. Henry lands at Milford Haven, vanquishes Richard III, and is declared King. He marries Elizabeth, and their union is blessed with the birth of an heir, Prince Arthur. This use of Henry VI, to suggest — as a future political solution — the programme subsequently followed by the first Tudor, is clearly intended to imply that the saintly king was a man of more than worldly wisdom: that he was, in fact, the *Divus henricus* with mystic powers bestowed by God.

The notion was taken a stage further by the story that he had actually predicted Henry Tudor's triumph. Bernardus Andreas writes that, on the death of Edmund Earl of Richmond, his young son, Henry, was summoned before the holy king who prophesied that one day the boy would take up the government of the kingdom and hold all authority in his hands. Then, thanks to the seer's inspired warning, the boy was able to flee across the sea and avoid the cruel sword of his enemies (Gairdner 1858: 14). The story is repeated by Polydore Vergil who remarks that King Henry VI, seeing the child and observing the 'haultie disposition thereof' assured the noblemen present, 'This trewly, this is he unto whom both we and our adversaryes must yeald and geave over the domynion'. And so the holy man showed how it would come to pass that 'Henry showld in time enjoy the kingdom' (Vergil, ed. Ellis 1844: 135).

Hall, in his classic exposition of the Tudor mission, repeats this story of the prophecy from Polydore Vergil: but with his customary ornamentation and added effectivenesses. Writing about the period immediately following Henry VI's restoration in October 1470, Hall describes how Jasper, Earl of Pembroke, went to Wales to collect Henry Tudor, son of his brother Edmund Earl of Richmond. This 'lorde Henry', Hall observes, was he who eventually gained the crown of England, 'whom wee ought to beleve, to be sent from God, and of hym onely to be provided a kyng, for to extinguish bothe the faccions and partes, of kyng Henry the vi and of kyng Edwarde the iiii'. Jasper took this boy to see King Henry who, remarking the youngster's wit and 'likely towardnes', made his momentous pronouncement:

Lo, surely this is he, to whom both wee and our adversaries levyng the possessyon of all thynges, shall hereafter geve rome and place. So this holy man shewed before, the chaunce that should happen, that this erle Henry so ordeined by God, should

in tyme to come (as he did in deede) have and enjoye the
kyngdome, and the whole rule of the realme.
                                        (Hall, ed. Ellis 1809: 287)

It is interesting that Hall — who was so antagonistic to miracles,
relics and all the trappings of popery, and who (as we shall see) rather
sneered at the attempt to have Henry VI's sanctity officially recognized —
felt that, within the context of his own vision of Tudor destiny, the
prophecy was worth repeating. Certainly, his version, subsequently
transmitted via Holinshed, kept the story going until Bacon repeated
it — albeit with a sceptical allusion to 'King Henry the sixth whose
innocency gave him holiness' — and Shakespeare incorporated it in the
third part of his *Henry VI*, where the monarch places his hand on the
head of the young Earl of Richmond whom he addresses as 'England's
hope'.

> ... If secret powers
> Suggest but truth to my divining thoughts
> This pretty lad will prove our country's bliss.
> His looks are full of peaceful majesty,
> His head by nature fram'd to wear a crown,
> His hand to wield a sceptre, and himself
> Likely in time to bless a regal throne.
> Make much of him, my lords; for this is he
> Must help you more than you are hurt by me.
>   (*Henry VI*, Pt.3, IV.vi)

Devout and divinely inspired; prophet, martyr and worker of miracles — the qualities of the defunct Henry VI constituted an irresistible
temptation. What could have been more desirable for Henry VII than
to have a Lancastrian saint as an uncle — especially one who had
predicted the Tudor triumph? And so began the laborious process for
the canonization of the murdered monarch.
    We do not know the precise date when the matter was first raised
with the Papacy, but it appears from a letter of Alexander VI, written in
October 1494, that there must have been a petition during the pontificate
of Innocent VIII — that is prior to July 1492 (Grosjean 1935: 168).
Alexander's letter asserts that, in issuing a commission to examine the
case for the canonization of Henry VI, the new Pope is following the
example of his predecessor, Innocent VIII. It is clear that Alexander is
replying to an initiative from Henry VII, for he states that the English
king had requested that a commission should be set up to enquire into
the miracles that had occurred through Henry VI's intercession and
into the popular pilgrimages and cures at his tomb. The Pope acceded,

and the commission included the Archbishop of Canterbury, John Morton, whose Episcopal Register contains a long document which probably relates to this business. It sets forth the various steps in the process of canonization; describes the necessary enquiries into the life, virtues and alleged miracles of the candidate; and provides an account of the ceremonies at Rome along with the relevant fees (Grosjean 1935: 167–76).

Subsequently, Henry VII petitioned the Pope for permission to remove the body of Henry VI from Windsor to Westminster, and the grounds for this request are rehearsed in a bull from Alexander. Henry VI, it declares, had been cruelly deprived of his kingdom and driven to a premature death. Yet Edward IV, not satisfied with this and wishing to extinguish his memory entirely, had caused the body to be buried in a remote place, Chertsey, in an unworthy tomb. Despite this, Henry's holiness had soon been manifested by miracles, and pilgrims began to visit his tomb so that Richard III – whose hatred had pursued Henry during his lifetime, and whose evil, cruel nature had destroyed every vestige of piety and humanity – then sought to suppress this public veneration by exhuming the body and having it reinterred at Windsor. Now it was claimed that the only fitting place for the mortal remains was at Westminster, in the Abbey Church where the kings of England were crowned and where many of them were buried. It was, moreover, the most important meeting place for the nobles, prelates and royalty of England, besides being the most widely celebrated site amongst other nations. Therefore it was requested that the bones and relics might be transferred to the place where people could visit the tomb and where the martyred king's merits could be made more famous (Grosjean 1935: 176–8).[46]

The plan for the removal of the body resulted in a petition for this purpose by the Abbot and Convent of Westminster, which the King referred to his Chancellor and Privy Council. On 26 February 1498, the various pleas were heard in a vigorous three-cornered contest (Grosjean 1935: 180–94). First, the Abbot of Chertsey claimed back the body on the grounds that Richard III had taken it to Windsor by violence without the consent of the Convent; that, therefore, the removal had been illegal; and that it should be returned forthwith. On the other hand, the Dean and Chapter of Windsor alleged that Chertsey had not only agreed to the removal of the body but also that the Abbot himself had assisted at the exhumation – 'manus suas proprias volunterie apposuit'. Finally, the Abbot of Westminster played his trump card by bringing numerous aged and obviously unreliable witnesses to prove that Henry VI himself had chosen to be buried at Westminster. Even the most ancient of these claimed to remember in great detail what Henry had said some forty years previously. One, Phyllyp Ilstowe –

aged about ninety — claimed that he distinctly remembered a visit of
Henry VI to St Edward's shrine at Westminster when the King had
remarked, 'Forsoth and forsoth, here is a good place for us'; and his
evidence was corroborated by a youngster of seventy-six, Richarde
Heryng, who reported the King's words as 'Forsothe, here woll we
lye'. Moreover, the Abbot's case continued, the Abbey Church was the
burying place of the kings of England and of the ancestors of Henry VI;
while the King had himself been a parishioner.[47]

The case was not long in dispute. On 5 March, the Council at
Greenwich decided in favour of Westminster and by 26 July the
project was under way. There still exists the indenture between Henry
VII and George Fawcett, Abbot of Westminster, for the removal of the
body from Windsor to Westminster where it was to be buried in the
Chapel of our Lady: 'the which Chapell oure said soverain Lord
entendith to make and bilde of new and in the same, not ferre from his
uncle, to be buryed himself' (Grosjean 1935: 200–1). The expense of
the project is enlarged upon, and the King insisted that the Convent
should contribute five hundred pounds towards the costs. In fact,
payment of the sum in 1501 is recorded in the account of John Islip,
Sacrist of Westminster; and, at about this time, preparations for the
building of the new chapel were set afoot. We know that, early in 1503,
to make room for the foundations, the existing chapel at the east end of
the High Altar was pulled down together with an adjacent tavern,
appropriately called the White Rose (Thomas and Thornley 1938:
321). There also survives, in the Cottonian Manuscripts at the British
Library, a drawing on vellum of a tomb entitled, *The monument intended
for Kinge Henry the Sixte* (see Fig. 12) This identification is in a later
hand: but the drawing itself appears contemporary, its design is very
much in the style of the rest of the fabric and it has even been attributed to Robert Vertue, master mason of Henry VII's chapel (Lethaby
1925, 164–6).

While all this controversy and activity were going on, enquiry continued
into the all-important miracles allegedly wrought by Henry. The direct
result of this investigation is still to be seen in the large manuscript
volume (now Royal Manuscript 13.C.VIII) prepared for John Morgan,
Bishop of St David's. This contains some 174 cases, the earliest dated
1481 and the latest 1500 — the latter year probably seeing the completion
of the volume. At the beginning of each miracle there are marginal
notes repeating the name of the location or county where the act was
supposed to have occurred; and then comes a Latin note as to whether
or not the miracle had been proved: *Probatum*, *Non reperitur*, *Non
est inventus*, and *Nullius effectus*. This investigation was left incomplete
and it has been suggested that, since the majority of the miracles
re-examined are those of children who would have been adult in the

Fig. 12. Design for a monument intended for Henry VI. British Library MS. Cottonian Augustus II.i.

next generation, the revision must have taken place in the reign of
Henry VIII, and that the breach with Rome caused the project to be
abandoned.[48]

However, we know that, on the death of Alexander VI, Henry VII
renewed his petitions to Pope Julius II and that a new commission –
consisting of Warham, who had succeeded Morton as Archbishop of
Canterbury, and the Bishops of Winchester, Durham, and London –
was appointed to continue the enquiry. Naturally, a new committee
would re-examine the relevant material already collected together; and
a letter from the Pope, in May 1507, shows that a petition had been
made to appoint delegates to study the evidence and that it was
considered necessary, in view of the age and condition of some of the
witnesses, to visit those who could not present themselves to give
testimony. Julius granted permission, made the appropriate arrange-
ments, and asked that the results should be forwarded to him (Grosjean
1935: 205–16). This was most likely the re-examination embodied in
the marginal notes in the miracles manuscript; and the interruption
came perhaps with the death of Henry VII. At that time the whole
matter was still at issue, and the very last reference to Henry VI, in this
reign, is in the King's will, which mentions the proposed translation of
the body to Westminster. This business, like that of the canonization,
had not been accomplished; and it never was.[49]

It seems strange that, despite Henry VII's keen interest and the
continuous efforts made during his reign, nothing was achieved. Edward
Hall, looking back on all this from the standpoint of the Henrician
Reformation, explains the failure as due simply to expense – 'Canonizing
of sainctes is costly', he jeers. The charges made at Rome for canonizing a
king were such that Henry VII 'thought it more necessary, to kepe his
money at home, for the profite of his realme and countrey, rather than
to empoverish his kingdom, for the gaining of a newe holy day of sainct
Henry: remitting to God, the judgement of his will and intent' (Hall,
ed. Ellis 1809: 304). But it is hard to reconcile this with the years of
negotiation, investigation and compilation which had been lavished on
the cause. Furthermore, in 1494, Pope Alexander VI had appointed a
commission – the same as that for investigating Henry VI – to
enquire into the character and miracles of Anselm, formerly Archbishop
of Canterbury. In this case the commission's favourable return resulted
in Anselm's canonization for which the expenses were paid by the
King; and it does not seem likely that Henry VII would have been
averse to paying even a much larger sum for the canonization of his
Lancastrian predecessor, if the Pope had favoured the proceedings
(Grosjean 1935: 118, 155, 169, 176).

Bacon, taking a more judicious and less jaundiced view of the
episode, is probably nearer the mark. He feels that Henry VII was

earnestly desirous 'to bring into the House of Lancaster celestial honour' by seeking the canonization of Henry VI, especially 'in respect of his famous prediction of the King's own assumption to the crown'. Bacon clearly implies political intention on the part of Henry VII. If Henry VI were indeed a saint, then the potency of his alleged prophecy would have been increased and would, in turn, have strengthened belief in the Divine inspiration of Henry Tudor's political success. Bacon then specifically rejects the general opinion that Julius II's price was too high. His own view is that the Pope was extremely jealous of the dignity of the Holy See and, 'knowing that King Henry the Sixth was reputed in the world abroad but for a simple man, was afraid it would but diminish the estimation of that kind of honour, if there were not a distance kept between innocents and saints' (Bacon, ed. Spedding 1858: 233–4). In view of the similar failure of earlier English attempts to gain canonization for Thomas of Lancaster and Edward II – both of whom were clearly unworthy of an honour which was being sought mainly as a political expedient – there is much to be said for Bacon's suggestion. It was papal policy rather than Henry Tudor's parsimony which prevented the canonization of Henry VI.

In the Vatican manuscript of Polydore Vergil's *Anglica Historia*, there is a story that the dying Henry Tudor asked his son to continue with the canonization process. During the Reformation this episode was carefully pruned from the history, and it does not appear in any of the first three printed editions (Hay 1952: 122). But even if the exhortation were uttered, it had no effect on Henry VIII who did almost nothing about the matter which was not raised again until 1528. Then suddenly it popped up during the difficult negotiations at Rome with regard to the divorce. Henry's ambassadors wrote to Wolsey that they had mentioned the canonization of Henry VI to the Pope who had answered that he would be well content to make a short process therein, but that the evidence would have to be examined in Rome, 'requyring a nombre of Cardinalls therat, with other ceremonies'. He said, therefore, that if Warham and Fox – who had already investigated the whole question – would send the process to Rome, as their commission required, the sentence of canonization would soon be passed (Strype 1822: I.ii, 107–8, 167–8). It is by no means clear why, after so long a period of neglect, the subject should have been raised at this juncture. Perhaps, in view of current difficulties with the Papacy, it was felt that it might be useful to have a saint in the family: though it is difficult to see what purpose this could have served. Whatever the reason, the canonization scheme is not mentioned again in this correspondence, and it does not occur elsewhere.

Most of the interest in Henry VI's sanctity – at least on the highest political level – seems to have died with Henry VII. There is, however, a scatter of evidence to show that popular devotion continued until Henry VI went the way of most saints in England during the 1530s. Evidently, his reputation was sufficient to gain him a place amidst a display of British sanctity in a pageant of the Assumption of the Virgin, prepared as part of the London entry of Henry VIII and the Emperor Charles V in 1522. This, the last scene of the series, was built at the little conduit in Cheapside, like a heaven shining with sun, moon and stars, populated not only with angels and the twelve apostles but also with Saint George, John the Baptist, and 'seynt Edmunde Kyng, seynt Edwarde Kyng and confessor, Kyng Henry the vj[th] with certayn bisshoppes sayntes off englonde, as seynt Dunstane, seynt Thomas off Cantorbury and seynt Erkenwolde' (Withington 1918: 178). Henry VI was mingling here with distinguished company: and it was the nearest he ever came to canonization.

It was also one of his nearest approaches, after death, to Westminster – although the 'image of Holy Kyng Herry', which was painted and gilded in September 1514 at the Savoy Hospital, was geographically closer. In Henry VIII's will there is provision that 'the Tombes and Aultars of King Henry the Sixth and also of King Edward the Fourth, our great Uncle and Graunfather, be made more Princely in the same place where they now be at our Charges' (Brewer 1862–1932: XXI.ii, no.634). It is unlikely that the warrior prince had ever felt much personal enthusiasm for his pious and ineffectual predecessor; while any lingering significance had, of course, been dissipated by the Reformation. And it is ironic that, in Henry VIII's last words on the subject, the erstwhile candidate for canonization, Lancastrian martyr, and prophet of Henry Tudor's success, should have been linked forever with the Yorkist king responsible for his persecution and death.

No less ironic, and even more revealing of the precise nature of Tudor regard for Henry VI, is the fulfilment of another, better-documented, dying wish of Henry VII. In his will there is a reference to the building of the chapel of King's College at Cambridge. This, it is remarked, was begun by Henry VI, a man 'of great holiness of life'; and there is a bequest of £5000 for the completion of the work together with a provision that, if this sum were to prove insufficient, then the executors should deliver, 'as moch money above the said V.M[1]. as shall suffice for the perfite finisshing and perfourming of the said works, and every parte of theim'. The money was not adequate. In 1513 a further £5000 was provided; and another two decades passed before Henry VIII paid for the completion of the work and all the interior fittings (Woodman 1986: 134–215; Colvin 1963–82: 187–95). The chapel had begun as a work of piety by the Lancastrian Henry VI. It had been continued first by his Yorkist adversary Edward IV, then by his alleged Yorkist murderer Richard III, and next by his Lancastrian

successor, Henry Tudor. Finally it was completed by Henry VIII, and —
smothered in roses, greyhounds, portcullises and dragons — it has
been transformed into a brilliant celebration of the Tudor dynasty (see
Fig. 7 above). The piety of its founder had become irrelevant.[7]

When the distinguished London printer, Richard Grafton, in his
Chronicle at Large (1569), came to sum up the character of Henry VI,
he followed closely — as was his wont — the words and imagery of
Edward Hall. There was, however, one significant omission. Hall,
prior to offering his explanation for the failure of the canonization
process, writes that the Lancastrian King's patience in adversity, for-
giveness in the face of the injuries heaped upon him, and 'other like
offices of holyness' caused God to 'worke miracles for him in his life
tyme (as old menne saied)'; and this was the reason why Henry VII
sought to have him canonized 'as other sainctes be' (Hall, ed. Ellis
1809: 304). The whole of this passage, together with the process
at Rome, is omitted by Grafton. After the Henrician Reformation,
Henry VI's career survived as a matter of historical record rather than
as an emotional, or even political, commitment. Despite the passing
allusions of chronicler and playwright, his prophecies belonged to the
past and his sanctity had become ideologically unacceptable. Even the
dynastic connection represented by Henry VI, as the last Lancastrian
monarch before the dubious appearance of Henry Tudor, seemed less
important than it had once been; and it is doubtful whether many
people, apart from those versed in heraldic lore, remembered the
original significance of the portcullis and greyhound. The 'rose both
red and white' was, however, a different story.

Chapter Four

THE ROSE BOTH RED AND WHITE

In 1548, Richard Grafton issued the first edition of a chronicle compiled by his friend — the lawyer, politician and enthusiast for the Reformation and all things Henrician — Edward Hall who, like the King he so admired, had died during the previous year. In Hall's chronicle, Henry is depicted as the flawless hero of a huge historical drama. His early years are a succession of masques, plays, disguisings and tournaments; his wars are simply an extension of this pageantry; his policies are triumphant; and his enemies are subdued. He reaches maturity by destroying the fleshly priest and villain of the drama, Cardinal Wolsey; and he fulfils his divine destiny by setting religion along the paths of righteousness, extirpating the Papacy, and creating the Church of England.

Hall's work was conceived as a monumental literary tribute to the King who, in his own person, resolved all the troubles which had beset England throughout the previous century. For Hall, history was no random concatenation of accidents. It was purposive; its direction was clear, inexorable and God-given; and the whole shape of the events which concerned England in the mid-sixteenth century was encapsulated in a suitably grandiose and comprehensive title:

> The union of the two noble and illustre famelies of Lancastre & Yorke beeyng long in continual discension for the croune of this noble realme, with all the actes done in bothe the tymes of the prynces, bothe of the one linage and of the other, beginnyng at the tyme of Kyng Henry the Fowerth, the first aucthor of this devision, and so successively proceading to the reigne of the high and prudent prince Kyng Henry the Eight, the undubitate flower and very heire of both the sayd linages.

In this first edition the title is displayed between two square fluted columns, surmounted by a picture of the King in council. The walls of the chamber are decorated with tiny roses, and the backcloth of the dais, on which the King sits enthroned, is adorned with two rose trees — one on each side of the throne. The engraving is on a very small scale and although, on close scrutiny, the images are clear enough, the decorative features are minimalist and the whole effect is neither imposing nor strikingly relevant to the book itself. For the second edition, however, in 1550, Grafton prepared a new title page which offers a simple and memorable pictorial summation of Hall's theme (see Fig. 13). This time the title is printed within a central box surrounded by two rose trees — one springing from John of Gaunt and the other from Edmund Langley, Duke of York — wending their way up both sides of the page until they unite in the marriage of Henry VII and Elizabeth of York who are seen, with their right hands clasped, emerging from their respective roses. Finally, at the top of the page, is Henry VIII, whose 'triumphant reigne' is the culmination of the title, picture and text. The rose imagery is taken up, again pictorially though less obtrusively, at the start of each new reign in the initial letters which are inscribed about the royal arms, supporters and badges of all the English monarchs (excepting Edward V and Richard III) from Henry IV to Henry VIII.

Transmitted by the various editions of Hall's work itself, by later chroniclers who borrowed from him, and most effectively by Shakespeare's history plays, the 'Wars of the Roses' and their dynastic resolution have become one of the most familiar of our historical notions. But the origins and development of the rose image under the early Tudors are less straightforward than Hall makes them appear.

Soon after the Battle of Bosworth, a contemporary chronicler described it in allegorical terms. The white roses of York (the sons of Edward IV), done to death by the boar (Richard III), had been avenged by the red rose (Henry VII) (Fulman 1684: I, 576). This imagery does not seem novel to us because, since the time of the Tudors, it has been customary to refer to the white rose of York and the red rose of Lancaster as though these symbols had been common currency throughout the struggle between the two houses. Yet it is difficult to adduce more than scanty evidence for this idea and, as far as we can tell, only the Yorkist party made much use of the device. Indeed, it was even argued by one distinguished nineteenth-century historian that the whole business was a Tudor invention and that the Croyland continuator was the first writer to mention the red rose (Ramsay 1892: 48, 133, 551). This is not strictly true, but it is not too much of an overstatement. The use of this symbol following the accession of Henry VII — and especially the use of the union rose, after his marriage — was, like the *British History*, a development of an established Yorkist theme.

The rose had never been an uncommon heraldic emblem. Numerous early examples may be found on seals and on rolls of arms; and, while the device was often adopted without any apparent special meaning by a particular family such as the Darcies, it is likely that, had such a

Fig. 13. Title page of Edward Hall's *The Union of the two noble and illustre famelies of Lancastre & Yorke* (1550).

family become the head of a faction in some major political brawl, then the emblem would have been used to signify their party. This is precisely what did happen to the Yorkists during the fifteenth century. The source of their device is unknown, though it was said of the Duke of York, Edward IV's father, that the 'Bages that he beryth by the castle of Clyfford is a Whyte Roose' (Ellis 1814: 226–7). Whatever the truth of this connection between the Cliffords and the rose, there is no doubt that the Yorkists made consistent use of the badge. Edward Plantagenet, second Duke of York, showed a rose of five leaves on his seal in 1403; Richard, the third Duke, displayed an ornamental shield of arms surmounted by a rose on his seal in 1436; and his widow, Cicely Neville, included a branch of roses beyond the armorial supporters of her seal in 1477 (Birch 1887–1900: III, nos.12,674, 12,712, 12,093). But it was the third Duke's son, who came to the throne as Edward IV, who made the greatest show of roses prior to the Tudor era.

During the contest with the house of Lancaster, Edward, as Earl of March, was frequently referred to as the 'Rose', and the symbol was sufficiently well known to become a commonplace in the spate of political poetry celebrating his deeds.[51] In the troublous year 1460, after the Yorkist victory at Northampton, one poet enthused:

> And ensaumple here of I take witnesse,
> Of certayne persones that late exiled were,
> Whos sorow is turned into ioyfulnesse,
> The Rose, the Feterlock, the Egle, and the Bere.

All these were well established heraldic badges of the Yorkist party: the Rose was Edward himself; the fetterlock was his father; the Eagle the Earl of Salisbury; and the Bear the Earl of Warwick. Another poem probably written in the same year, dealing with the relative positions of the rival parties and the policy to be pursued by the Yorkists, has several references to Edward as the Rose which, springing 'in wyntre so fresshe', is a wonderful sight to see. Again, after the Battle of Towton in March 1461, a poet used the rose as a symbol for Edward, making it the basis of his paean of joy at the Yorkist victory:

> Now is the Rose of Rone growen to a gret honoure,
> Therefore syng we euerychone, I-blessid be that
> > floure.

Four years later, as Edward consolidated his power, the theme was developed:

> An R. for the Rose that is frische and wol nat fade,
> Bothe the rote and the stalke that is of grete honour
> from normandie vnto norway the leues do springe,
> from irlonde vnto Estlonde me reioise that floure.

Edward's increasing authority was similarly celebrated in another poem, *Edwardus, Dei Gratia*, which asserted that his 'stoke', or family tree, had long lain dead, but that God had caused Edward to spring forth to be head of all England:

> Sithe god hathe yeuen the, thorough his myghte,
> Owte of that stoke birede in sight
> The floure to springe, a Rosse so white,
> Edwardes, Dei gracia.

In Wales, where, as we have seen, Edward was greeted as a descendant of Gwladys Duy, the Yorkist party may also have become identified with the white rose symbol, because Lewis Glyn Cothi, exulting in the prowess of Sir William Herbert and his service to the Yorkist cause in the north of England, describes how he had 'triumphed with white roses'. Finally, on Edward's death, the rose featured amongst his chief emblems in a poem of mourning:

> O noble Edward, wher art thowe be-come,
> Which full worthy I haue seen goyng in estate?
> Edward the iiij[th] I mene, with the sonne,
> The rose, the sonne-beme, which were full
> fortunate:
> Noon erthly Prince durst make with hym debate.
> Art thow agoo, and was here yesterday?
> All men of England ar bound for thee to pray.

This popular identification with the rose was perpetuated in Edward IV's seals and coinage. All his seals, apart from the first, show a rose or *rose-en-soleil*. The fourth is the most beflowered, depicting, on the obverse, the King's head surmounted by a rose with, to the right, a shield of arms placed beneath a rose while itself surmounting a sun and rose. The shield on the left has a large and a small rose over it, and a sun and rose below; while the field at the base has a sun on the right and a rose on the left. The reverse has a field diapered lozengy, and the spaces are charged alternately with sun and rose (Birch 1887–1900: I, nos.301–17). Edward's coinage confirms that the rose was regarded as the principal Yorkist emblem, for the halfpenny, half-groat, groat, half-angel, angel, quarter-rose-noble and half-rose-noble

Fig. 14.   Noble coin of Edward IV (Hocking no.751).

all incorporate the flower in some part of the design. Most magnificent
of all was the rose-noble or ryal. The noble had, from the reign of
Edward III, shown on the obverse the figure of a king standing in a
ship. Now Edward IV's noble has a full-blown rose by the side of the
traditional ship, with its standing figure of a king holding sword and
shield; and the reverse depicts a floriated cross with a rose in the
centre of a sun of sixteen rays (see Fig. 14) (Hocking 1906: nos.619,
751–72). Since both Edward V, in his brief reign, and Richard III
continued the rose tradition in their seals and coinage, it is clear that,
whatever the position of the Lancastrians with regard to the badge,
there was undoubtedly a Yorkist rose over which they could triumph.[52]

That the rose was occasionally regarded as a Lancastrian symbol
prior to 1485 is suggested by a poem of the Anglesey bard Robin Ddu
who, writing during the exile of the Tudors, looked forward hopefully
to the time when red roses would 'rule in splendour' (Evans 1915: 8).
Nevertheless, the rose of Lancaster does not figure in the surviving
political verse of the period as does the rose of York. Nor do Yorkist
poems dwell on the antagonism of the roses: which, if the Lancastrians
were commonly associated with the emblem, is a curious omission.

It is equally difficult to establish a convincing heraldic tradition for
the red rose of Lancaster, although it is sometimes said that the flower
had first been introduced into England by a son of Henry III, Edmund
Crouchback, Earl of Lancaster, who imported it from Provins where
he had resided on his return from Palestine (Stanley 1882: 165–6).
This tale has not been substantiated but, by the middle of the sixteenth
century, it was evidently accepted as, for example, in an illuminated
genealogy deriving Elizabeth I from Rollo, where the Lancastrian line
of descent from Edmund is accompanied by red roses, and the scroll
containing biographical information about Edmund himself is overgrown
with the flower. This genealogy decorates the Yorkist line with white
roses, deriving them from Edmund Langley, son of Edward III (British
Library MS. King's 396, fols.24–5).

The later Lancastrian use of the badge is only slightly better documented. Matilda daughter of the third Earl of Lancaster and Maud Chaworth, showed a rose in the centre of her seal of 1347; and Henry Plantagenet, Duke of Lancaster, included roses on his seals between the years 1351 and 1362. John of Gaunt did not have the rose on his seals: but the curtains of the bed he bequeathed to St Paul's were made of cloth of gold powdered with golden roses, tuns and white ostrich feathers — a decoration recalling one of the vestments mentioned in the will of the Black Prince. Henry of Lancaster, afterwards King Henry IV, had on his seal as Duke of Lancaster sprigs of broom (the *planta genista* alluding to his surname), and cinquefoil roses were only included in the design along the edge as ornaments, while neither Henry V nor Henry VI made much of the rose emblem. It is true that, in a Tudor manuscript dealing with heraldic banners and badges, the rose is drawn to indicate 'Henry the V for the bage of lanchester', and a banner attributed to the same king is decorated with an heraldic antelope argent, Henry's dexter supporter, on a field powdered with ten roses. But these drawings almost certainly represent a reading-back of mid-sixteenth-century usage into the history of the House of Lancaster. On the other hand, among the various vestments bequeathed by Henry V to churches in France, there were three 'Capas de velvet rubeas, cum rosis aureis, leonibus, & floribus de liciarum, brouderatas', which suggests that, like the lion and fleur-de-lis, the rose may have been considered a royal badge.[53]

Scattered references such as these prove nothing, and it was only with the accession of Henry VII that the red rose became prominent as a symbol of the triumphant House of Lancaster. The reason for this was probably twofold. In the first place, there may have been some connection between Lancaster and the rose — hinted at in Robin Ddu's poem — the details of which now elude us; and secondly, the white rose had become the most popular symbol of the Yorkist party and would have suggested the red rose as appropriately emblematic of Henry's victory. In fact, this is how the Croyland continuator employed the rose in his report of the Battle of Bosworth, and much the same idea appears in a poem, *Rose of England*, written some time before 1495.[54] Here England is described as a beautiful garden in which there had grown a fine red rose — a crowned king of England, Ireland and France.

> Then came in a beast men call a bore,
>   And he rooted this garden vpp and downe,
> By the seede of the rose he sett noe store,
>   But afterwards itt wore the crowne.

The boar tore up the rose branches and buried them under the clay, but a branch was preserved and remained in exile until the time was ripe for its return. 'Att Milford haven he entered in' and, in the ensuing Battle of Bosworth, Richard III was slain. England had been through troublous times, but now the garden flourished anew, its flowers fragrant and beautiful:

> Our King, he is the rose soe redd,
>   That now does fflourish ffresh and gay.
> Confound his ffoes, Lord, wee beseeche,
>   And loue his grace both night and day.

The red rose is used here to represent Henry VII and the House of Lancaster in the same way that Edward IV had been represented by a rose in earlier political poetry. What we do not know is whether this alludes to an established Lancastrian tradition or whether it is simply a response to the pre-existent Yorkist emblem.

From the beginning of Henry VII's reign, the red rose was used for decorative purposes. In the *Empcions* for his coronation there are various payments relating to a special 'trappour of the Rede Roses', to a 'dragon and rede roses of a trappour' and to a 'trappour of blue velvete with rede roses with gold of venys and dragons fete werke' (Legg 1901: 203−5, 210). However, it is impossible to say whether these references indicate any conscious attempt to cultivate the red rose as a counterblast to its Yorkist rival because, on this occasion, it is only one badge among many. It is also impossible to be precise about a potentially more interesting reference in the great inventory of tapestries, taken at the death of Henry VIII. One of the items was a 36 metre 'pece of Arras of the *Komyng into England of King Henrye the VII* taking with th'one hande the crowne from King Richard the thirde, usurper of the same, and with th'other hand holding a roose crowned' (Thompson 1906: 171, 268, 356). Unfortunately, the tapestry does not survive, and there is no other information.

Much more important than the single rose was the 'rose both red and white', symbolizing the union and joint inheritance of the houses of York and Lancaster, and it was this symbol which, more than anything else, strengthened the idea that there ever had been a red rose of Lancaster. On Christmas Day 1483, in the cathedral of Rennes, the exiled Henry Tudor had taken an oath that, as soon as he became king, he would marry Elizabeth, eldest daughter of Edward IV: a promise repeated on 10 December 1485 in response to a request of the Commons through their Speaker. The marriage took place on 18 January 1486. Yet, by an indenture of 4 November 1485, when Sir

Giles Daubeney and Bartholomew Reed (a leading London goldsmith) were appointed master-workers at the royal mint, the first issue of Henry VII's coinage had already been put in train and the Ryal showed, on the reverse, a small shield bearing the arms of France, over a double rose (Challis 1978: 44−5, 52). This, presumably, was in anticipation of the forthcoming marriage and, when contrasted with the single roses included in the design of Edward IV's Ryal or Rose-noble, its meaning is clear (see Fig. 10 above).

The badge remained a favourite device on coins throughout the Tudor era, just as Henry VII's use of the rose on his great seal set the fashion for his successors whose seals all incorporated the flower in some part of their design. Henry Tudor's seal includes on the obverse, at the King's feet, two roses slipped and leaved; and on the reverse the field is diapered lozengy with a fleur-de-lis at each point of intersection and a rose in each space. Henry VIII's first seal was from the same matrix as that of his father; but his second (from 1532 to 1541) and third (1542−7) both show on the reverse the King in armour, riding on a horse whose caparison is diapered with fleur-de-lis and a large rose surrounded by foliage on the border; while in the field of the seal, above the horse's tail, is a large *rose-en-soleil*. Double roses also feature on the reverse of Edward VI's second seal and on both sides of his sister Mary's second seal: though in the latter case it is accompanied by castles and pomegranates alluding to the Queen's Spanish descent through her mother, Katharine of Aragon. On the joint seal designed for Philip and Mary, roses dwindle to a minor decorative element on the caparison of the Queen's horse and in the background to the equestrian portraits on the reverse; but they return to prominence on Elizabeth's first seal and, even more strikingly, on her second seal despite its departure, in other respects, from traditional imagery (see Figs. 2, 15−18).[55]

Yet, for all its popularity and ubiquity, the genesis of the union rose as a badge remains mysterious. We do not know who thought it up, and − apart from its inclusion on Henry VII's Ryal and the other gold coins of his first issue − we do not know how it was so speedily spread abroad. Less than two months after the marriage with Elizabeth of York, the King began his first provincial tour of the middle and northern parts of his realm. The city council of York had started to arrange for the royal visit early in March, when they agreed that some 'convenyent Shew' should be prepared and that the parish priest of Spofforth, Henry Hudson − who had previously distinguished himself by organizing a *syght* for the visit of Richard III in August 1483 − should be put in charge of the matter. Amongst the York Civic Records there survives a detailed programme for the reception showing that the first pageant, at the city gate, was to be like a heaven surmounting a

Fig. 15. Great Seal of Henry VII.
Engraving from Sanford 1677, 456.

Fig. 16. Great Seal of Edward VI.
Engraving from Sanford 1677, 458.

world devoid of inhabitants but filled with trees and flowers. The whole scene was to be a mechanical contrivance in which a red rose would be joined by a white and then, when they were united, all other flowers would bow before them to acknowledge their sovereignty, 'shewing the rose to be the principall of all floures, as witnesh Barthilmow, and therupon shall come fro a cloud a croune covering the roses'. Hudson's conception was ingenious. Utilizing stage machinery already available from York's mystery plays, and developing a hint from the famous encyclopedist, Bartholomaeus Anglicus, concerning the supremacy of the rose, he mixed it all together as a celebration of the marriage between York and Lancaster.[56]

If actually presented, this pageant would have been the first public allusion to the union of the roses; and it has recently been argued that the York dignitaries were influenced in their ideas about the royal entry by their dealings with the King, and that these ideas may be traced in the correspondence between city and monarch (McGee 1989: 29–34). This is certainly the case with regard to York's general professions of loyalty which had been encouraged by Henry's diplomacy; and it is obvious that the devisers of the show would also have been acutely aware of the need for relevance. There is, however, no evidence to suggest that any details of theme or imagery were specifically suggested by the King or by those close to him. Naturally, it remains possible that such suggestions were offered: but it is also possible that Henry Hudson had simply been visited by a flash of inspiration.

Thereafter, roses continued to appear as a matter of course in the occasional pageant series prepared for English royal entries. In the joint entry of Charles V and Henry VIII in 1522, for example, the rose was used to represent the Tudor dynasty in a scene devised by the versatile John Rastell. This pageant included an elaborate mechanism depicting the Island of England set amidst the sea and filled with animals, birds, fish, trees and flowers; and, as King and Emperor drew near, 'the bestys dyd move and goo, the fisshes dyd sprynge, the byrdes dyd synge rejoysing the comyng of the ij princes'. There were also two articulated images, one 'lyke to the emprowr in visage' within a castle signifying Castile; the other 'lyke to the kynges grace' in an arbour appropriately filled with roses. The next pageant in this series, at the great conduit in Cheapside, also featured a rose – this time a great flower, not fully blown, which descended and opened 'litill and litill', until a maiden stepped forth holding two roses, a red and a white. The first she offered to Henry but, since she offered the white rose to the Emperor, the symbolism of the scene seems unfocused and imprecise (Withington 1918: I, 177–8).

Another variation of the union rose, less confused though somewhat debased by application to the King's paramour, appeared during Anne

Boleyn's entry into London in 1533 when the pageant at Cornhill offered a scenic paraphrase of the new queen's badge. Anne's device was a stump of a golden tree floreated with the roses of York and Lancaster. On this was the white falcon of Ormond, holding in his dexter claw a sceptre tipped with the fleur-de-lis, the whole surmounted by a crown of England. In the pageant this badge was represented by a 'rote of golde' planted on a little mountain set with red and white roses. From the heavenly root above the scene, a white falcon descended, settled on the roof, and was crowned by an angel while a child recited:

> Behold and see the falcon white,
> How she begynneth hir winges to spred,
> And for our coumforte, to take hir flight!
> But where woll she sease, as you doo red?
> A rare sight, and yett to be joyed,
> On the Rose, chief floure that ever was,
> This bird to light, that all birdes dothe passe!
> (Furnivall 1868–72: I, 376)

Anne's career was soon over and her falcon was briefly replaced by Jane Seymour's phoenix, though neither Jane, nor any of the next three queens who assumed the unenviable role of Henry VIII's wife, was accorded a pageantic entry into London; and it was not until the coronation of Jane's son, Edward VI, in 1547, that there was another pageant series when the nine-year-old boy was hailed as a 'redolent rose', a 'flourishing flower', and as 'the only cause of amity and concord'. One of the scenes prepared for him was, like that for Anne Boleyn, a variation on a badge, with the phoenix of the Seymours descending and settling on a mount flowering with white and red roses, gillyflowers and hawthorns (Nichols 1857: I, cclxxxv–cclxxxvi). There is no record that roses were alluded to in the pageants for Mary in 1553 or for Philip and Mary in the following year; but when Elizabeth I made her pre-coronation entry into London in 1559, not only was there an explicit statement of the original dynastic theme but it was also hammered home in the account printed by Richard Tottel less than a fortnight after the event.[57] The first pageant of the series was built across Gracious Street and consisted of three stages set one above the other. On the lowest level, beneath a cloth of estate, were figured Henry VII within a red rose, and Elizabeth of York within a white rose: 'And these personages wer so set, that the one of them joyned handes with thother, with the ring of matrimonie perceived on the finger'. From each flower sprang a branch and these, being united, passed up into the second stage where Henry VIII, 'which sprong out of the former stocke', was seated next to Anne Boleyn, 'mother to our

Fig. 17. Great Seal of Philip and Mary.
Engraving from Sanford 1677, 459.

Fig. 18. Second Great Seal of Elizabeth I.
Engraving from Sanford 1677, 460.

most soveraign ladie quene Elizabeth that now is'. Finally, the roses continued to the uppermost level where Queen Elizabeth I sat enthroned. In the foreground of the pageant was inscribed its title, *The uniting of the two houses of Lancastre and Yorke*; the whole structure was covered with red and white roses and sentences relating to the idea of unity; and a child recited explanatory verses to the Queen.

> The two princes that sit under one cloth of state,
> The man in the red rose, the woman in the white:
> Henry the .vii. And Queene Elizabeth his mate,
> By ryng of mariage as man and wife unite.
> Bothe heires to both their bloodes, to Lancastre the king
> The Queene to Yorke, in one the two houses did knit,
> Of whom as heire to both, Henry the eyght did spring,
> In whose seat his true heire thou quene Elsabeth doth sit.

> Therfore as civill warre, and shede of blood did cease
> When these two houses were united into one
> So now that jarrs shall stint, and quietnes encrease,
> We trust, O noble Queene, thou wilt be cause alone.

'Unitie', says Tottel's pamphlet, 'was the ende wherat the whole devise shotte'. The pageant recalls, both in title and form, the frontispiece of the 1550 edition of Hall's *Union of the two noble and illustre famelies of Lancastre & Yorke* and it can scarcely be coincidental that Hall's publisher, Richard Grafton, was prominent among the committee appointed by the London authorities to prepare Elizabeth's entry. The pageant at Gracious Street was virtually a topical, three-dimensional reworking of the woodcut (see Fig. 13).

Twenty years later similar imagery was still being used to introduce the civic pageantry prepared for Elizabeth's visit to Norwich (McGee and Meagher 1981: 100–2). It had been intended that the Queen should be greeted just outside the city by its founder, King Gurgunt, who was to explain something of the history of England and draw parallels between ancient achievements and modern – notably those of the first Tudors.

> When doubtfull warres the British Princes long had wroong,
> My grandsire first uniting all did weare the crowne.
> Of Yorke and Lancaster, who did conclude the broyles?
> Thy grandsire Henry Seventh, a king of great renowne.

Similarly, Gurgunt was to continue, just as Brennus once sacked and half destroyed ancient Rome, so Elizabeth's 'puissant father' had dealt with 'new Rome that purple whore'. This speech was not delivered because a shower of rain caused the Queen to hasten on to the city gates which had been 'enriched and beautified'. On the front were the Queen's arms; to one side but slightly lower, was an escutcheon of St George; on the other side were the arms of the city; and directly beneath the royal arms was a falcon with the motto, 'God and the Queene we serve'. The inner side of the gate was adorned with a red rose signifying (according to the pamphleteer who recorded all this information) 'the house of Yorke', and a white rose 'representing the house of Lancaster'. Was this a mere slip of the pen due to haste? Or does it reveal crass ignorance, no less suggestive of the limitations of imagery than Stephen Gardiner's earlier misinterpretation of the royal seal (see above, pages 17−19)? At least there could be no mistake about the white and red rose united in the middle. This, 'expressing the union', surmounted the Queen's arms and the following lines:

> DIVISION kindled stryfe,
>   Blist UNION quenchte the flame:
> Thence sprang our noble PHAENIX deare
>   The pearlesse Prince of FAME.

Elizabeth's visit to Norwich was the last Tudor royal entry, and more than ninety years separated it from Henry VII's visit to York and the production of Henry Hudson's masterpiece. Yet the handling of the image of the roses, with its straightforward message of dynastic union and peace, had scarcely altered. This is not surprising since Tudor civic pageantry was, in the main, unsophisticated and intellectually stagnant. But what of rose imagery in the upper echelons of society?

Most of the earliest surviving evidence occurs within a courtly context where the idea of union was quickly reduced to a visual and literary formula. In the manuscript of Giovanni de' Giglis's *Epithalamium de nuptiis*, for example, the two roses are shown intertwining around the arms of England supported by a white greyhound. Similarly, Petrus Carmelianus's poem, describing the resolution of England's troubles by the marriage of York and Lancaster, introduces its theme in a frontispiece illustrated with red and white roses, together with the royal arms supported by a greyhound and dragon. The union of the roses also passed into music during Henry Tudor's reign when Sir Thomas Philips used it in a part song celebrating Prince Arthur.

> b) The rose it is a ryal floure
> c) The red or the white? Shewe his colour.
> a) Both be full swete and of lyke savoure
> b) All on them be

> That day to se,
> It lykyth well me.
> c) I love the rose both red and white.
> a) Is that your pure perfite appetite?
> b) To here talk of them is my delite.
> c) Joyed may we be
>   Oure prince to see
>   And roses three.
>   (Stevens 1961, 364−5)

Arthur was not the only union rose celebrated by the poets and musicians, since each of Henry VII's children by Elizabeth of York could be represented in the same fashion. The marriage of the Princess Margaret to James IV of Scotland not only prompted Walter Ogilby to praise her as the most precious rose, but it also provided the illustrious William Dunbar with a pretext to perpetrate his *Thistle and the Rose* in which the poet is exhorted by the Lady May to write in her honour. He obliges with a story of Dame Nature who, having commanded every bird, beast and bloom to appear before her, makes the lion king of beasts, the eagle king of birds, and the thistle, 'kept with a bush of spears', king of flowers. The thistle is enjoined to guard all his subjects but especially the fresh rose 'of colour red and white' for she is the most perfect of all flowers:

> So full of blissful angelic beauty,
> Imperial birth, honour and dignity!

Finally the rose is crowned and receives the homage of the whole kingdom of flowers in a manner reminiscent of the York pageant of 1486.

> A costly crown, with clarified stones bright.
> This comely Queen did on her head enclose,
> While all the land illumined of the light:
> Wherefore, methought, all flowers did rejoice,
> Crying at once, Hail, be thou, richest Rose!
> Hail, herbs' Empress! Hail, freshest Queen of Flowers!
> To thee be glory and honour at all hours.
>   (Arber 1901: 34−40)

Prince Henry − especially after the death of his brother Arthur − was similarly eulogized. For example, Stephen Hawes, a groom of the Chamber, presented a long poem, *The Example of Virtue*, to Henry VII in which the King is himself the Red Rose 'regally sprung' from a noble stock and root. The White Rose, long assailed by 'tempests troublous' was now 'fortified and made delicious' for:

> It plesed GOD for him so to provide,
>   That his redolent buds shall not slide;
>   But ever increase and be victorious
>   Of fatal briars, which be contrarious.

God caused the two roses to be combined in marriage, and from this joint root was sprung Prince Henry who is one day to be King of England.

> O, noble Prince HENRY! Our second treasure,
>   Surmounting in virtue and mirror of beauty!
> O, gem of gentleness and lantern of pleasure!
>   O, rubicund blossom and star of humility!
>   O, famous bud, full of benignity!
>   I pray to GOD well for to increase
>   Your high Estate in rest and peace.
>   (Arber 1901: 217 ff.)

Henry VIII fulfilled Stephen Hawes's prophecy. He was the union rose appointed by God to succeed his father to the throne and, from the beginning of his reign, poets and musicians harped upon this theme. Skelton, hoping for some preferment on the basis of having been Henry's tutor, begins *A lawde and prayse made for our sovereigne lord the kyng* with just such an allusion:

> The rose both white and Red
> In one Rose nowe dothe grow:
> Thus thorow every stede
> There of the same dothe blow:
> Grace the sede did sow:
> England, Now gaddir flouris
> Exclude now all dolouris.

He declares that the virtues and qualities of Alexander, Adrastus, Adonis, Priam King of great Troy, and Mars himself are combined in the person of the young King Henry, and that the iniquities of the past shall be amended as Justice herself, Astraea, 'Shall now com and do Right' (Skelton, ed. Henderson 1948: 131−2). Astraea was later to be pressed into regular service for Elizabeth I and she had earlier been associated with Henry VII by the Latin poet Johannes Opicius (Gairdner 1858: lxi). But Skelton suggests that Justice, in the guise of Astraea, had been absent from England until the advent of Henry VIII; and this implied criticism of Henry VII's governance is repeated in another more substantial courtly manifestation, the *Great Tournament Roll of Westminster*, a pictorial record of the tournament held in February 1511, to celebrate the birth of a short-lived son and heir to Henry VIII. This 18 metre vellum roll concludes with a picture of a large crowned union rose accompanied by a poem stressing that an age of gloom and misery has now passed, and, like Skelton's *lawde*, the opening verse alludes to the rose theme:

> Oure ryall Rose now Reignyng rede and Whyte
> Sure graftyd is on grounde of nobylnes
> In harry the viij our Ioye and our delyte
> Subdewer of wronge mayntenar of rightwysnes
> Fowntayne of honer exsampler of larges
> Our clypsid son now cleryd is from the darke
> By harry our kyng the flour of nateurs warke.
>
> (Anglo 1968: I, 106)

As in the previous reign the idea was set to music, and one noteworthy production is a manuscript preserved in the Royal Collection (British Library Royal MS.11.E.xi). This has, at the beginning, a Latin poem of seventeen elegiac couplets in honour of Henry VIII, the union of the erstwhile rival houses of York and Lancaster, and, symbolically, the union of the roses. The poem is written within the framework of three rose trees — one red, one white and, in the centre, a crowned union rose — growing from a castle built on a sea-girt island. This setting is itself a concise emblematic compendium of the marriage of Henry VIII and Katharine of Aragon: the wall surrounding the island has four towers, two surmounted by banners with the cross of St George, one with the arms of England, and the other with those of Castile and Aragon; on one side of the island there is a pomegranate tree; the castle itself is flanked by a dragon or wyvern, and a white greyhound; and in the open gateway, beneath a portcullis, there sits a lion. On the following page the poem is inscribed with music on two carefully drawn circular staves (Bassus and Contratenor) enclosing roses; and there follows the music by 'M[agister] Sampson' (see Figs. 19 and 20).

Personal tributes of this kind always remained in vogue because the union rose, along with the other dynastic badges, provided a ready means whereby any offering — whether from subject to monarch or from monarch to subject — could be Tudorized and made relevant. But the double rose, unlike the other heraldic symbols, referred not only to lineage but also to the peace which resulted from the union of York and Lancaster, and it occurs so frequently — generally in trivial

Fig. 19. Tudor badges in British Library MS. Royal 11.E.xi, fol.2^r.

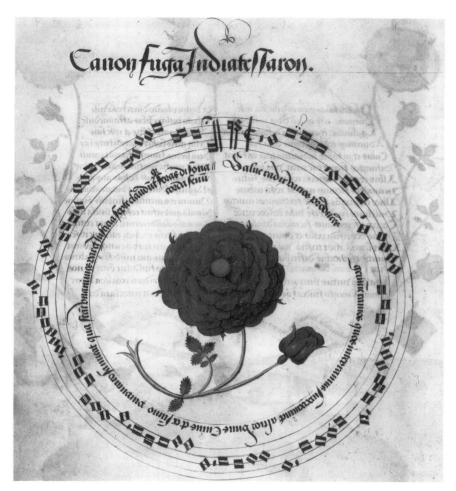

Fig. 20. The rose in British Library MS. Royal 11.E.xi, fol.2ᵛ.

contexts, but sometimes in works of enduring merit — that it is impossible to do more than cite a few illustrative examples.

When Elizabeth visited Windsor in 1563, the title-page of the presentation volume of complimentary Latin verses by the youthful Etonians was ornamented with the royal arms and the Tudor rose. In the same way, when she visited Woodstock and Oxford in August 1566, the occasion was commemorated in another manuscript of complimentary addresses by the members of the university, introduced by a drawing of the royal arms within a garter, flanked on one side by a crowned rose and on the other by a crowned portcullis.[58] Manuscripts such as these were intended for the monarch's personal scrutiny and the devices were nothing more than allusive decorations; but woodcuts in printed books could give images a wider circulation and could carry a more specific political meaning, as we have already seen in the title-page of Edward Hall's chronicle. Another suggestive occurrence is in the dedication to Foxe's *Actes and Monuments* where the initial letter *C*, enclosing a portrait of the Queen, is wreathed about with the two roses of York and Lancaster which eventually unite above the royal head — a piece of typography which proved so attractive that it was reused in two other printed books (see below, page 121 and Fig. 27).

In Spenser's *Shepheards Calender* (1579), where the April Eclogue is 'purposely intended to the honor and prayse of our most gracious sovereigne, Queene Elizabeth', the royal cheeks display the 'Redde rose medled with the White' — a rather less heraldic and bizarre conceit than Fulke Greville's 'red and white rose quartered in her face'[59] — and the image is provided with a careful historical 'Glosse'.

> By the mingling of the Redde rose and the White is meant the uniting of the two principall houses of Lancaster and Yorke; by whose longe discord and deadly debate this realm many yeares was sore traveiled, and almost cleane decayed. Til the famous Henry the seventh, of the line of Lancaster, taking to wife the most vertuous Princesse Elizabeth, daughter to the fourth Edward of the house of Yorke, begat the most royal Henry the eyght aforesayde, in whom was the first union of the Whyte rose and the Redde.

More than a decade later the same theme received its most famous expression, when Henry Tudor, as Duke of Richmond, appeared on the London stage to renew his promise to marry the Yorkist heiress.

> And then, as we have ta'en the sacrament,
> We will unite the white rose and the red:
> Smile, heaven, upon this fair conjunction,
> That long hath frown'd upon their enmity!
> What traitor hears me, and says not amen?
> England hath long been mad, and scarr'd herself;
> The brother blindly shed the brother's blood,
> The father rashly slaughter'd his own son,
> The son, compell'd, been butcher to the sire:
> All this divided York and Lancaster,
> Divided in their dire division,
> O! now, let Richmond and Elizabeth,
> The true succeeders of each royal house,

By God's fair ordinance, conjoin together;
And let their heirs — God, if thy will be so, —
Enrich the time to come with smooth-fac'd peace,
With smiling plenty, and fair prosperous days!

The context of this speech, at the end of Shakespeare's *Richard III*, remains impressive, and the words are memorable. But the historical sentiment was a century-old commonplace. An evocative political hieroglyph, the union rose, was virtually conterminous with the Tudor dynasty and, in the sophisticated courtly milieu as in the cruder tradition of civic pageantry, it never changed. This is not to suggest either that Elizabeth's admirers did not have at their disposal a thesaurus of other metaphors, or that they were unable to move from the red and white rose to variants, such as the eglantine, more personal to the Queen whom they sought to please. As George Peele, proclaiming England's joy on the Queen's birthday, exhorted:

Wear eglantine,
And wreaths of roses red and white put on
In honour of that day, you lovely nymphs,
And paeans sing and sweet melodious songs.
(Peele, ed. Bullen 1888: II, 344)

The *union* rose, however, remained precisely what it had always been: a double flower, celebrating the peace which had come to England through the marriage of York and Lancaster. It was the symbol *par excellence* of the Tudor dynasty's historical mission. And this is how it appeared in *An Elegie upon the death of the high and renowned Princesse, our late Soveraigne Elizabeth*, written by one, John Lane. Lane's principal claim to posthumous renown is that he knew Milton's father; but he expresses, with surprising poignancy, the demise of the Queen, the end of a dynasty, and the death of an image.

For loe, the Flower which was so fresh and gay,
And made November like another May,
How daintily so ere it did compose
The beautie of the white and crimson Rose,
The Flower is parcht, the silken leafe is blasted,
The Roote decay'd, and all the glory wasted.
(Hazlitt 1875: II, Item ii)

Chapter Five

IMAGE MAKING: THE MEANS AND THE LIMITATIONS

Immediately after his triumph at the Battle of Bosworth, Henry Tudor began to make his way across the country to London. He proceeded, 'like a triumphing general', wrote Polydore Vergil, and everywhere he was greeted with the greatest joy.

> Far and wide the people hastened to assemble by the roadside, saluting him as king and filling the length of his journey with laden tables and overflowing goblets, so that the weary victors might refresh themselves. But when he approached the capital, the chief magistrate (whom they call the 'mayor') and all the citizens came forth to meet him and accompanied him ceremoniously as he entered the city: trumpeters went in front with the spoils of the enemy, thundering forth martial sounds.
>
> (Vergil, ed. Hay 1950: 2−5)

The whole progress and entry is made to sound like a Roman triumph: but this is probably more the effect of Polydore's Italian humanist vision than of any conscious classical imitation by Henry and his followers. At any event, this was the first public appearance of the Tudor dynasty. It was also, for the great majority of ordinary folk who made up the cheering roadside throng on the way to the capital, probably the last time that they ever saw their monarch in the flesh. And this is the nub of the problem.

Opportunities for the ceremonial exposition of kingship in Renaissance England, as elsewhere in Europe, were varied. The symbols and signs of monarchy were displayed on great state occasions, during progresses and processions, and at solemn entries and court festivals. Emblems were circulated on coinage and on seals; they decorated palaces, chapels, pavilions and tombs; and they adorned paintings, tapestries, jewels and other works of art. The imagery of kingship could be proclaimed from the pulpit, and it could be set forth in books, both in words and pictures. The means *seem* comprehensive enough: yet a moment's reflection reveals their limitations and transience. A distant view of Henry VIII or Elizabeth I in a procession may have been an exciting, even awe-inspiring, experience. Possession of an image of the sovereign may have been a comfort, especially if it were graven upon a coin. The sheer size of a palace and the opulence of its decoration may have been an impressive evocation of monarchical power. But not one of these things was likely to help a lay observer understand the significance of Constantine and Henrician Caesaro-papism or to resolve the mysteries of the sieve, serpent or ermine.

Coronations and funerals

The public appearances of the English monarchy were not designed to purvey such ephemeral and concocted political theories or emblematic conceits to the nation. Their primary symbolic function was to affirm the abstract permanence of kingship, although this — accompanied as it was by the magnificently apparelled figure of the ruler, either alive or in effigy, and by heraldic and genealogical display — inevitably served also to affirm dynastic legitimacy.

The extent to which the major ceremonies were concerned with eternal political verities (or at least those so deemed by contemporaries) is made clear by the continuity of coronation ritual despite the Reformation and despite the unprecedented demands made on the organizers of state occasions by the accession of queens regnant as opposed to queens consort. There was, it is true, an oil change — when Mary, worried that the holy chrism had been contaminated at the sacring of her Reformist brother, Edward, requested a fresh supply from her uncle, the Emperor Charles V — but little else of significance was altered.[60] Even more revealing, especially of the way in which these ceremonies soared above transient dynastic concerns, are the records relating to the coronation of Henry Tudor. One of these, *A litle devise of the coronacion of the most high and mightie christian Prince Henrie the vijth* — a detailed formulary of the ceremonial — was not only closely modelled on the fourteenth-century *Liber Regalis* and the fifteenth-century *Forma et Modus* but was, in fact, so hastily adapted from a document originally prepared for the coronation of Richard III, that many of the nobles who served on that earlier occasion still figure as participants. Indeed, the *Litle devise* assumes that the King will be crowned together with a queen — as was the case with Richard III — and at various points in the proceedings Richard's name has simply been struck through and replaced by Henry's.

The traditional character of the ceremony itself, with its rigidly prescribed order of service, anointing and presentation of the regalia, is confirmed by the contemporary narrative of the occasion which omits all details 'because thei be sufficiently recorded at Westminster'. The only personal aspects of the sequence of events which made up the coronation celebrations were heraldic. During the creation of the knights of the Bath on the evening prior to the coronation, Henry instituted a new pursuivant called *Rougedragon* in allusion to his British descent; in the procession from the Tower to Westminster Hall the horses of the royal henchmen were trapped with 'divers arms and badges of the King'; and, when the King's Champion delivered his customary challenge at the coronation banquet, his horse was covered with a 'riche trapper of Cadewaladras armes' (Anglo 1960).

The coronation, for all its splendour and symbolic significance, was not normally the first great public spectacle of any reign. Paradoxically, this position was occupied by the final exit of the previous monarch, when it was customary for the heir to be proclaimed after the royal corpse had been laid to rest. The heralds would then remove their tabards; hang them on the rail of the hearse; solemnly proclaim that the deceased was indeed dead; and, having resumed their coats, appeal for long life to be granted to the new monarch. This was the procedure for all the Tudor kings and queens apart from the founder of the dynasty himself who had not inherited the crown from anybody. Moreover, the last rites of his immediate predecessors had been singularly unpropitious. Edward IV, it is true, had been decently interred (Wall 1891: 343−51): but his son and heir, Edward V, had been murdered and secretly buried. So, too, had the last Lancastrian, Henry VI; while Richard III travelled on his cortege, bloodstained and naked, slung across the back of a horse, and his conqueror was obliged to have himself proclaimed on the field of battle. Henry VII's will makes provision for his own funeral, asking that his executors should have a special respect to the laud of God, the well-being of his soul, and 'somewhat to our dignitie Roial', avoiding, however 'dampnable pompe and oteragious superfluities' (Wall 1891: 365). In the event, Henry's obsequies set a prodigious standard of magnificence and confirmed − even if they did not actually establish − the dynastic display deemed appropriate for such occasions.

He died on 21 April 1509 at Richmond Palace where his body remained for over two weeks while masses and dirges were performed. Then on 9 May the embalmed, lead-encased and encoffined corpse was placed on a chariot covered with black cloth of gold. On the coffin rested a life-size 'Picture' − that is an effigy − of the late King,

> crowned and richly apparreled in his Parliament Roobe, bearing in his Right Hand a Scepter, and in his Left Hand a Ball of golde, over whome ther was hanginge a riche Cloth of golde pitched upon Fowre Staves, which were sett at the Fowre Corners of

the said Charett, wich Charett was drawen with Seaven great Coursers, trapped in Black Velvett with the Armes of England on everie Courser set on bothe Sydes.

(Leland 1770: IV, 304)

On either side of each courser walked a knight carrying a banner; and at the corners of the chariot walked four barons each carrying a banner of the 'Kyngs *Avowries*' or patrons — the Trinity, Our Lady, St George and Mary Magdalene. Unfortunately, the banners borne by the knights are not specified in the contemporary records, but Edward Hall later reported that Henry VII's chariot was 'garnished with banners and Pencelles of tharmes of his dominions, titles and genealogies' (Hall, ed. Ellis 1809: 506): and this heraldic and genealogical mode is corroborated by the evidence of many other obsequies. Among the funeral expenses for Prince Arthur, for example, in 1502 there was payment for twelve bannerols of 'divers armes devised by garter', including not only the prince's own arms and those of Wales, Cornwall and Chester, but also those of Cadwalader and Brutus; at the funeral of Henry VIII there were 'twelve banners of descents'; for Anne of Cleves there were 'bannerols of her armes and dyscentes'; and for Queen Mary there were 'great Banners of Damaske of the Quenes Desents'.[61] Early in the seventeenth century, Nicholas Charles, Lancaster Herald, sketched the 'Standards and Banners of Kinge Henry the Eight' which still survived at St George's Chapel Windsor — where Henry VIII had been buried — and he showed three standards (dragon, greyhound and lion), three banners (St George, a crowned figure of Henry VIII with sceptre and orb, and another figure of the Virgin Mary and child), and two banners showing the arms of his grandparents (Edward IV with Elizabeth Woodville), and his parents (Henry VII with Elizabeth of York) (British Library MS. Lansdowne 874, fol.49).[62]

The chariot bearing Henry VII's mortal remains and robed effigy set out for St Paul's accompanied by a great throng of prelates singing the office for the dead, household officers and servants and other mourners totalling more than 1400 persons, together with nearly 700 torchbearers. When they reached St George's Fields, near Southwark, they were met by another enormous group of London civic dignitaries and religious fraternities so that, in the end, the cortege included all the Lords, temporal and spiritual, all the judges and councillors, representatives of Florence, Venice, Portugal, Spain, France and the 'Esterlings' and virtually everybody of political, religious and juridical significance in the kingdom. The coffin and effigy were placed under a hearse of wax in the choir of St Paul's, and a solemn requiem was sung. The following day, after mass, John Fisher, Bishop of Rochester, preached a sermon which was subsequently printed by Wynkyn de Worde — a unique example of royal funerary publication in sixteenth-century England.[63] After the sermon, the coffin and effigy were removed in similar state to Westminster where they were set beneath another wax hearse — the most 'costly and curious Light possibly to be made by Mans Hands, which was of xiii principal Stonderds, richly decked with Banners'. The next day witnessed the final ceremonies when there were three masses; and it was at the last of these — the Requiem sung by the Archbishop of Canterbury — that the obsequies reached their climax which was more heraldic than liturgical.

> First there came Twoe Herauds in their Cotearmours unto the Duke of Buckingham, beinge Chiefe Mourner, kneelinge at the West End of the Herse, goinge before him, from the Herse unto the Place where the Archebishop stoode to take the Offeringe; where he, representinge the Kyngs Person, offered a Testamente of Golde: Which done the said Herauds conveyed him againe to the Place he came frome. Then the said Herauds came in like Manner unto the Earle of Arondell and unto the Earle of North-umberland, and conveyed them unto a Knight which stoode beside the Herse, holdinge the Kyngs Cotearmoure. Of whom the said Herauds received the said Cotearmour, and delivered it to the said Twoe Earles; which solempnly bearinge the said Cotearmour betwene them offered it up unto the said Archebishop with great Reverence; the which he received and delivered unto a Bishop, which delivered it over unto an Heraud standinge even by them on the South Side of the Churche; which done the said Herauds conveyed the Twoe Earles againe unto theire Places.
>
> (Leland 1770: IV, 306–7)

And so the process of heraldic offerings continued: the coat armour followed, one after the other, by the late King's shield, sword, helmet, and then his 'goodlie Courser, trapped in Black velvet, with the Armes of England embrothered upon the same'. After this, again under the supervision of the heralds, the nobles laid palls of cloth of gold across the royal corpse, 'as thick as they might lie', before the last offering of the King's great banner and standard. The Bishop of London preached a noble sermon, the palls were removed, the effigy was taken to St Edward's Shrine, the coffin was revealed and lowered into the vault, the great officers of state cast in their batons, and, at last, the heralds proclaimed 'Le noble Roy, Henri le Septieme est mort' and, immedi-ately thereafter, 'Vive le noble Roy Henri le Huitiesme'.

Again, as was the case with Tudor coronations, there was little fundamental change in the pattern of the royal funeral. There was no need for it. Naturally, at the funeral of Edward VI the four great banners of the King's *Avowries* were abandoned in favour of banners displaying the Order of the Garter, the Red Cross, the arms of Edward's mother and of the Queen Dowager. And, just as naturally, the religious banners were restored for Mary's funeral before disappearing once again at Elizabeth's cortège. All the rest — the immense procession (that for Henry VIII was estimated as four miles in length), the heraldic and genealogical display, and the huge chariot with the coffin and effigy — remained largely intact. This we can see from the records of that last Tudor funeral at Westminster on 28 April 1603 when the cortège included standards of the dragon, greyhound and lion; banners of Chester, Cornwall, Wales, Ireland and England; and 'The Chariott drawne by foure Horses upon which charret stood the Coffyn covered with purple velvett and upon that the representation. The Canopy borne by six Knights.' On either side of the chariot were six nobles carrying twelve bannerols displaying the arms of the Queen's royal ancestors impaling the arms of their wives: Henry II and Eleanor of Aquitaine, John and Isabel of Angoulesme, Henry III and Eleanor of Aragon, Edward I and Eleanor of Castile, Edward II and Isabel of France, Edward III and Philippa of Hainault, Edmond of Langley, Duke of York and Isabel of Castile, Richard Earl of Cambridge and Anne Mortimer, Richard Duke of York and Cicely Neville, Edward IV and Elizabeth Woodville, Henry VII and Elizabeth of York, Henry VIII and Anne Boleyn (Nichols 1788: II). These genealogical bannerols, clustered around Elizabeth's funeral chariot, constituted the final and most emphatic statement upon the enduring frailty of Henry VII's claim to the throne. Beyond her grandfather, the royal lineage of Elizabeth Tudor was wholly Yorkist (see Fig. 21).

Royal funerals were immensely lavish and dramatic and, though scarcely more personalized than the coronations, their ceremonial was rather more familiar — not because rulers died more frequently than they were crowned, but because queens consort and princes and princesses were also interred with great pomp, even when the deceased was still in his first year, as was the case with Henry VII's third son Edmund in 1500, or had lasted only fifty-one days, as had Henry VIII's first-born, Henry, in 1511. Moreover, in addition to the family funerals of the Tudors themselves, the citizens of London would have had many opportunities to witness heraldic obsequies: of foreign potentates such as the Emperor, and the kings and queens of France, Spain and Denmark; of great lords both temporal and spiritual: of lesser gentry and of important city dignitaries. However much the funerary rites differed in scale — with the number of 'morners of estate', for example, strictly allocated according to rank and ranging from sixteen for a king

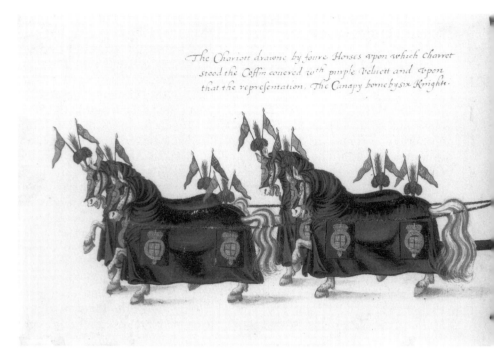

Fig. 21.   Funeral car of Elizabeth I showing her effigy, banners and canopy. British Library MS. Additional 35,324, fol.37ᵛ.

down to two for a merchant — there was little significant variation either in ritual, the offering of weapons and coat armour, or in the overwhelmingly heraldic nature of the imagery.[64]

   The most interesting feature of royal funerals was the lifesize image of the deceased, modelled from the death mask and used as a practical solution to the problem of protracted display of the cadaver. One poet, Henry Petowe, lamenting the death of Elizabeth, dwelt on the evocative power and verisimilitude of her funeral effigy.

> Oh, yee spectators, which did view that sight!
>   Say, if you truelie say, could you refraine,
> To shed a sea of teares in deathes despight,
>   That rest her hence, whome Art brought backe againe?
>   He that knew her, and had Eliza seene,
>   Would sweare that figure were faire England's Queene.

Indeed, Petowe adds, a man of judgement — not knowing that she were dead, and seeing her lying thus in her rich robes, crowned with

sceptre in hand — would have sworn, 'To Parliament rides this sweet slumbring Maide' (Petowe 1603).

The theoretical position, as viewed from a modern standpoint, has been succinctly stated by Ernst Kantorowicz.

> Enclosed in the coffin of lead, which itself was encased in a casket of wood, there rested the corpse of the king, his mortal and normally visible — though now invisible — body natural; whereas his normally invisible body politic was on this occasion visibly displayed by the effigy in its pompous regalia: a *persona ficta* — the effigy — impersonating a *persona ficta* — the *'Dignitas'*.
>
> (Kantorowicz 1957: 421)

The custom was exported from England to France where its theoretical implications were gradually elaborated and made explicit. However, in England the whole business remained characteristically vague and inconsistent. Perhaps the most suggestive example of the use of the funeral effigy was at the reburial of Richard Duke of York at Fotheringay Castle in 1476. The Duke had been slain at the battle of Wakefield sixteen years previously, and his head had been impaled on the gates of York with a crown of paper in an ugly mockery of his regal pretensions.

When, at the instigation of his widow Cicely, his bones were ceremoniously reinterred, the coffin containing his remains was surmounted by 'an Image like to the Prince lieng uppright in a Surcott and a Mantle of blewe velvete furred with Ermyns'. On the effigy's head was 'a Cappe of Meyntenance with an Aungell standing in white holding a Crowne over his hed in Token that hee was kinge of right'.[65]

The notion of regal continuity was here strained to the utmost. The Duke could hardly be regarded as still theoretically alive and participating in his own funeral until the moment that his son might be proclaimed king by the heralds. The Yorkist position was simply that Richard, as king 'of right', *deserved* to have a proper funeral complete with a crowned effigy. Yet he had never been crowned, had never been anointed and had never reigned. The basis for honouring him with an effigy was no more than the need to make a political statement, coupled with a generalized sense of what was fitting. There is no evidence that anybody felt that regal rituals ought to be congruent and, in England, this vagueness persisted throughout the history of the heraldic funeral from the fifteenth to the late seventeenth century. If it is assumed, for example, that contemporaries seriously regarded such effigies as symbolic expressions of the immortality of the royal *Dignitas*, then why were queens consort such as Elizabeth of York and Jane Seymour represented at their funerals by similar effigies? Why had it been customary, in fifteenth-century England, to parade an effigy of a defunct bishop, clad in full pontificals and with all the insignia of his office, at his funeral? And, although this custom was allegedly outmoded in the following century — 'the figure is not nowe used' wrote one authority about the year 1560 — why was Bishop Stephen Gardiner's coffin surmounted by an effigy at his funeral in February 1556?[66] Contemporaries did not feel obliged to resolve such questions. The practice seems to have been a ritualistic gesture whose force was emotional and intuitive rather than ideologically precise; and it is just this kind of imprecision which makes solemn theoretical pronouncements on Tudor symbolism and ceremonial so suspect.

Progresses and other public spectacles

Coronations and funerals were the most imposing and most symbolically potent of all ceremonies of state. Not only were the lords temporal and spiritual physically present, but the Commons, too — at least in London and the home counties — were actively involved either in the customary pre-coronation procession from the Tower to Westminster, or as spectators when the mighty funeral corteges made their way from Richmond (Henry VII and Elizabeth I), Greenwich (Edward VI) or St James (Mary) to Westminster, or from Whitehall to Windsor via Syon, as was the case with Henry VIII. No other public spectacles could compare, either emotionally or ritualistically, with these. Processions to Parliament certainly involved the three estates, but they evoked little enthusiasm; and it is very striking that the ceremonies on these occasions were scarcely considered worthy of mention even by a London chronicler such as Edward Hall who was himself a Member of Parliament. Royal weddings and births were also events of dynastic importance which could afford opportunities for celebration at court and throughout the land. But Henry VIII's nuptials decreased in splendour as they increased in number; the last Tudor marriage was Mary's to Philip of Spain in 1554: and there was no Tudor birth after 1536.

When else did royalty display itself to the people? The Tudor progress, when the monarch and court left London and undertook gentle journeys through the countryside — sometimes staying at the royal palaces and sometimes being entertained by one loyal subject after another — is commonly described as an instrument of policy. This is undoubtedly true as far as it goes. The trouble is that the royal progress normally did not go very far. Henry VII, Henry VIII and Elizabeth I all travelled about a good deal; and it is true that there was often some correlation between the places they visited and the relative stability of the realm. This was especially marked, for example, in the case of Henry VII's first provincial tour when he set out for York 'in order to keep in obedience the folk of the North, savage and more eager than others for upheavals' (Vergil, ed. Hay 1950: 11), and when similar considerations induced Henry VIII to undertake a similar journey in 1541. However, the assertion that the progresses of Elizabeth I were 'the means by which the cult of the imperial virgin was systematically promoted' (Strong 1984: 77), is open to question.

The highpoint of Elizabethan eulogy — the fifteen years after the defeat of the Armada — coincides precisely with a marked decline in the geographical area covered by the progresses. In any case, the principal purpose of these royal peregrinations had always been rec-reational or prophylactic — riding, hunting and avoiding the London plague season — not political; and they were largely confined to the home counties, within comfortable travelling distance from London, and never too far from what was clearly recognized as the essential power base of the dynasty. The Tudor monarchy on the move may well have been a stirring spectacle, but only a tiny minority of English people ever saw it.[67]

Even more severe limitations may be noted elsewhere. The solemn entries of Renaissance rulers into their cities were occasions when *tableaux vivants*, speeches, triumphal arches or other architectural de-vices, paintings and inscriptions could carry a rich symbolism deriving from history, the Scriptures and classical mythology, all made more or less relevant to the visiting monarchs, their dynasty and current affairs. Tudor civic spectacle differed from its continental counterparts only in its comparative infrequency, poverty and the rarity of its classical imagery; and, like all such pageantry, its contemporary allusions conveyed more of the hopes, aspirations and fears of the citizenry than of the visiting monarch's political aims. These shows had as their principal object, *Laudando praecipere* − to teach by praising − but the princes, willing enough to make various *ad hoc* concessions and gestures of goodwill, were so eager to lap up the *laudando* that they generally paid little attention to the *praecipere* on which the citizens built their hopes for better government in the future.[68]

Nor is there anything to suggest that central authority in Tudor England ever dictated a programme for such pageantry or imposed rigorous supervision over its execution. The best illustration of this lack of control is the entry of Queen Mary and Philip of Spain into London on 18 August 1554: without doubt the most politically sensitive and difficult of all Tudor pageant series. Six months earlier Wyatt's rebellion had ended in disaster for all those implicated, and the Queen had expressed her hope that exemplary punishment of the guilty would purify the kingdom. Retribution was quick and copious. New gallows were set up at every gate and key point in London, and all were liberally festooned with the bodies of the executed − some hanged, some quartered and some decapitated. The Catholic reaction was under way and the Counter Reformation in England was soon sealed by the Anglo-Spanish marriage. It is remarkable, therefore, that when the Court of Aldermen met on 22 May to appoint a committee to plan 'such pageauntes and other open demonstrations of joye as they shoulde think meate to be made and sett furthe within the Cytie at the comminge of the prynce of Spayne', they decided to include Thomas Berthelet, who had been King's Printer under Henry VIII, and Richard Grafton who had held the same position under Edward VI. Berthelet had been responsible for printing, amongst much else, all the Henrician propagandist tracts by Richard Moryson and the anti-clerical works of Christopher Saint German; while Grafton, who had printed the Great Bible in 1539, had also printed the proclamation for Queen Jane in 1553, and had been deprived of his post as royal Printer by Queen Mary. Even as the aldermen met, the London streets were still disfigured by the gallows and rotting remains of the last display of Protestant defiance. Yet none of this deterred the city dignitaries from appointing men of noted reformist sympathies. And nobody interfered.

More startling still was the result of the committee's deliberations when their second pageant, set up at the conduit in Gracechurch Street, depicted the Nine Worthies augmented by Henry VIII and Edward VI, all armed with maces, swords or poleaxes, 'saving Henry the eight, which was paynted having in one hand a cepter and in the other hande a booke, whereon was wrytten *Verbum Dei*'. Again, nobody interfered. It was not until King Philip had witnessed the scene and passed on his way that Stephen Gardiner, Bishop of Winchester, having noted the Bible in the pageant-king's hand, summoned the painter, berated him with 'ville wourdes calling him traytour', and made him paint out the offending book. The poor artist hastily replaced it with a new pair of gloves, but was so fearful of leaving some part of the book and its reformist title in King Henry's hand that 'he wiped away a piece of his fingers withal'. The point of the story, both for the chronicler who reports it and for John Foxe who elaborates upon it, is Gardiner's hatred for true religion and especially of the Bible. The point of the story for us is that − given the general hostility to the Spanish marriage, the recent insurrection, the bloody public retribution, and the violence of the doctrinal context − the City of London could still appoint men like Berthelet and Grafton to plan a pageant series for their Catholic monarchs; that they could produce a pageant showing Henry VIII with the Word of God; and that it was not until *after* Philip had passed this scene that Gardiner noticed anything amiss and tried to do something about it (Anglo 1969: 324−30). This curious episode has recently been interpreted as though it establishes governmental censorship in relation to civic pageantry (King 1989: 101−2), whereas it suggests precisely the opposite. Clearly, until after the event, there had been no supervision or censorship whatever.

English civic pageantry was not the effective means of mass communication that its modern students (myself included, I regret to say) have sometimes deemed it to be. The cause of dynastic image-building was not well served when civic pageantry strayed beyond obvious political allusions and a straightforward exhibition of the customary repertoire of heraldic arms and badges. Esoteric and complex ideas were likely to lose the audience. In 1501, for example, there was, amongst much astronomical and cosmological imagery, a representation of Prince Arthur within the 'Sphere of the Sun' − a cosmic mechanism hinting at a solar apotheosis. The prince himself was identified both as Christ the Redeemer and Christ the Sun of Justice; while, in the following scene, Henry VII was depicted as God the Father. This seems heady and exciting stuff. Yet not one of the three surviving eye-witness observers (all of them otherwise competent and circumstantial) even hints at having an inkling as to what it was all about (Anglo 1963: 72−81). It is, moreover, a poor instrument of propaganda and communication which is experienced only once or twice in an entire reign. This 1501 entry was the solitary Tudor pageant series in London prior to the visit of the Emperor Charles V in 1522. The citizens of Lincoln, for their part, never saw Tudor pageantry or Henry Tudor himself after his visit in 1486; and those of Worcester only glimpsed him on one day thereafter. York had to wait until 1541 for its first and only view of Henry VIII; and Elizabeth's loyal Londoners would have had to cling to their memories of her entry in 1559 for the rest of the century, because there was no repeat performance.

On the other hand it is true that the monarch and the court could be seen in full splendour at tournaments — frequently in the early years of Henry VIII's reign, occasionally in the reigns of his father, son, and elder daughter, and once or twice a year in the reign of Elizabeth. Recently it has been asserted that these spectacular shows constituted events of 'high political seriousness'; that the 'microcosm of the realm provided by a crowded tiltyard on a tournament day was in itself a potent instrument of royal propaganda'; that the costly preparations 'were all part of a serious and far-reaching purpose'; and that 'national unity was perhaps nowhere better in evidence than in the provision of viewing stands for thousands of spectators, arranged so as to express the accepted social hierarchy' (Young 1987: 7, 74, 122). More specifically, the Accession Day tilts for Elizabeth I have inspired one distinguished historian to exclaim, 'what incredible spectacles they must have been, and what an impact they must have made at the time!'; such an impact, indeed, that the tilts became an 'integral part of the aesthetic milieu of the eighties and nineties'; 'everyone knew about them, everyone had seen them' (Strong 1977: 146, 151). Everyone who was a somebody, perhaps: but not everyone who was a nobody. In such exaggerated statements the intentional fallacy has been allowed to run riot. By stepping beyond the bounds of the courtly milieu to make more general assertions about national policy, they stretch, distort and ultimately destroy the fabric of their argument. That Henry VIII loved to disport himself within the lists is certain (see Fig. 22). That Elizabeth I enjoyed being celebrated as the Lady of the Tournament is likely. That all this was a deliberate plan to reproduce the social hierarchy in a court festival and thus somehow influence the nation is a misinterpretation arising from a conflation of three diverse elements: high-flown sixteenth-century theories concerning the 'effects' of the later Valois court entertainments, especially as enunciated by Balthazar de Beaujoyeulx;[69] a tacit and unwarranted assumption that these notions were shared by the Elizabethan intelligentsia; and an anachronistic belief in the power of mass manipulation by the media. Some historians write as though Renaissance Neoplatonic magic actually worked; or they give the impression that, all over England, Elizabethan fans were following the tournaments as if glued to television sets, sitting enthralled while expert commentators described the lists, interpreted the sexual and political significance of the Queen's apparel, analysed the courtly *imprese*, and assessed the prowess of the tilters. Yet how could the great

(a)

(b)

Fig. 22. (a) 'Tonlet armour' of Henry VIII, assembled in haste for the foot combat at the Field of Cloth of Gold, 1520.
(b) Foot combat armour from the royal garniture of Henry VIII, made in the Royal workshops at Greenwich under the Master Armourer Erasmus Kyrkener, dated 1540. The garniture can be assembled to make armour for the field, tilt, tourney, and foot combat.

mass of the Queen's subjects share in the spectacle, devices and verses which would have been largely incomprehensible and inaudible even to those actually present? Some of the citizens of London may have enjoyed these emasculated neochivalric spectacles but, apart from the fact that Elizabeth's Accession Day had become a national holiday, it is difficult to see how the rest of England would have been affected.

Much the same may be said of the annual ceremonies of the Order of the Garter. All the Tudors were concerned with these − from Henry VII who followed the example of Edward IV in resuscitating the Order, Henry VIII and Edward VI who carefully revised the statutes, Mary who re-revised them, and Elizabeth who, with typical ambiguity, enhanced the ceremonial while leaving it essentially unaltered. The Garter festival at Windsor Castle was a splendid courtly occasion and, in the latter half of Elizabeth's reign, even became something of a public spectacle. Breuning von Buchenbach, envoy of Duke Frederick of Württemberg, described the ceremonies of 1595 mentioning that 'there was a great crush in the chapel, as many of the common people had thronged thither'; and he also reports that the Queen, with her knights 'marched round the yard three times so that everyone could have a good view of them' (Klarwill 1928: 378). The questions remain: what was the population of England in 1595, and what proportion managed to squeeze into the chapel and courtyard of Windsor Castle?

State portraiture

The chances of ordinary Tudor citizens pondering the inner meaning of works of art was even more remote and, had they enjoyed such opportunities, the imagery was more likely to relate to some local dignitary than to the sovereign. Who actually saw the architectural embellishments, illuminated manuscripts, gems and paintings that are constantly before *our* eyes as evidence of Tudor iconography? None of these things was intended for the uncouth gaze of the multitude. Indeed, it is not always clear just whose gaze they were intended for or whose vanity they were supposed to flatter. There were, for example, a whole series of historical paintings at Cowdray House representing important occasions in the reign of Henry VIII: but they were probably acquired or commissioned by the owner of the house, Sir William FitzWilliam, because he had participated *with the King* in the various events thus celebrated, and not simply because Henry VIII figured therein (Anglo 1966: 304−7). Or consider the famous and oft-reproduced 'Procession' picture of Elizabeth I. Surrounded by courtiers, and covered by a canopy held by her nobles, the seated figure of the Queen appears to float in mid-air − though there can be no doubt that the ill-executed painting is intended to suggest some means of loco-motion. According to Sir Roy Strong, she is seated on some sort of wheeled vehicle pushed by one of the grooms of her Chamber, though this is not at all apparent to the untrained eye. All of this, we are told, is *Eliza Triumphans*: for the canopy links her procession thematically with that of Alphonso the Great at Naples in 1443, as depicted on the triumphal gateway of his castle; while, beyond that, links are further suggested with the ancient Roman emperors themselves. The picture, in this interpretation, becomes an icon of imperial monarchy and a central source for establishing that there was a 'cult' of Queen Elizabeth I (Strong 1977: 17−55).

However, although, in terms of rank, the Queen is certainly the most important figure in the picture, she is not the person being flattered here. Prominent in the foreground, and basking in the glory reflected on him by his proximity to the monarch, is the Master of the Horse, Edward Somerset, Earl of Worcester, and it is more reasonable to assume that the painting was executed to enhance the courtier's self-esteem rather than to distort it into an arcane allusion to the Queen's imperial destiny.

Moreover, the dialectical leap from mid-fifteenth-century Naples to late sixteenth-century England is implausible, and it is doubtful that the canopy was regarded as having a specifically imperial significance. It was, rather, a practical convenience − originally intended to protect distinguished personages from the sun or rain − which had developed into a ceremonial stage property. It can be seen depicted at Persepolis as a glorified umbrella protecting an Achaemenian monarch as early as about 521 BC (Roaf 1989: 35), and was still being used in similar fashion by the medieval popes and Venetian doges. Elaborated into a portable canopy, it was used in religious and state processions throughout Europe and was held over kings on solemn occasions such as coronations, entries and funerals. It was carried over English queens at least from the reign of Richard II, as we know from the *Liber regalis* of the late fourteenth century (Legg 1901: 100, 108, 122, 129); and it came in for special mention in 1509 when Katharine of Aragon, just passing a tavern called the *Cardinal's Hat*, on her way to be crowned with Henry VIII, was caught in so sudden and heavy a shower that the canopy born over her was not 'sufficient to deffend hyr ffrom wetyng of hir mantell' (Thomas and Thornley 1938: 340). Eventually, the canopy became so commonplace that it functioned simply as an indicator of high rank. Whether alive or dead, the person beneath it was easily recognized as the focal point of the ceremony. Canopies are mentioned in numerous narratives of state occasions and may be seen in many European illustrations of religious processions, royal entries and funerals, and even in a non-royal funeral such as that of Cardinal Wolsey (see Fig. 23).[70] Most pertinent are the thumbnail, contemporary pen and ink sketches of Elizabeth I herself *en route* to her coronation in 1559 (see above, page 30 and note 26). She rides on a horse-drawn litter, protected by the canopy; and proceeds in a manner more dignified than that depicted in the 'procession' painting − especially if this really does show her being trundled along on an invisible wheelbarrow, like a bejewelled sack of vegetables (see Fig. 24).

Portraiture has been a particularly tempting field for scholars who, possibly influenced by the richly documented decorative programmes for the palaces of continental princes, have sought to establish the existence of a coherent Tudor artistic policy. An instructive example of this, in relation to Henry VII, concerns the great hall of Richmond Palace, which was described in the only surviving contemporary account as follows.

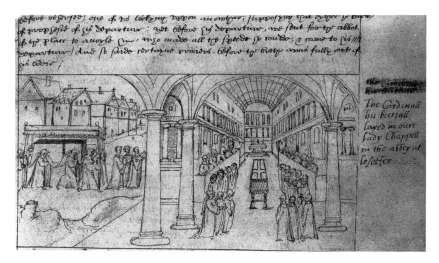

Fig. 23. A composite view of Wolsey's funeral, showing first the canopy and then his coffin laid in Our Lady Chapel in the Abbey of Leicester. Bodleian Library MS. Douce 363, fol.91^r.

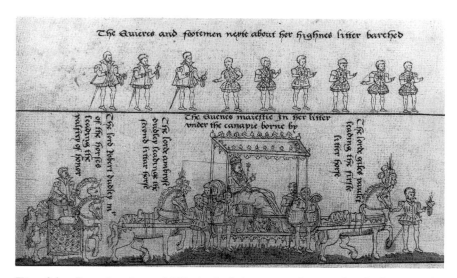

Fig. 24. Pen drawing of Elizabeth I in procession, a detail showing the canopy carried over her litter. College of Arms MS. M.6, fol.41^v. For the whole page, see Fig. 4 above.

In the wallys and siddys of this halle, betwene the wyndowes, bethe pictures of the noble kinges of this realme, in their harnes and robes of goold; as brute, engist, king William Rufus, king Arthur, king Henry and many othir of that name; king Richard, king Edward, and of thoes names, many noble waryours, and kinges of this riall realme, with ther fachons and swordes in theire handes, visagid, and apperyng like bold and valiaunt knightes; and so their dedis and actes in the chroniclis right evydently bethe shewen and declared. Emonge thes nombre of famous kinges, in the higher parte, uppon the left hond, is the semely pictur and personage of our moost excellent and heyghe suffrayn now reignyng uppon us, his liege people, Kyng Henry the vijth, as worthy that rumme and place with thoes glorious princes, as eny king that ever reigned in this lond.

(College of Arms MS. 1st M.13, fol.62')

On the basis of this description it has been suggested that the 'pictures' were designed, probably by the King's painter, Maynard, 'according to the familiar three-quarter bust formula developed by Rogier van der Weyden'; that an observer's eye, travelling along the two lines of wall portraits, 'inevitably rests at the hall's focal point at the higher end where the King's throne stands'; that there, high above the throne, is the picture of Henry VII himself, 'illuminated by light from all the windows and receiving the homage of all the other portraits of past kings'; and that the entire arrangement and composition of these 'portraits' thus constituted the 'first recorded attempt to portray the Tudor monarchy as a font of magnificence, the chief of the Burgundian virtues'.

Nor is this all. The contemporary account went on to mention that the walls of the hall were 'hongid with riche clothes of Arres their werkys representyng many noble batalles and seages, as of Ierusalem, troy, albe, and many other'. This is interpreted as a deliberate attempt to establish a chivalric Burgundian context, and it is asserted that 'while the rows of portraits converge on the image of Henry that dominates one end of the great hall, so the tapestries focus upon the throne beneath that portrait' (Kipling 1977: 60–1). A glance at the Tudor text itself, however, shows how far a preconception – that the decoration must be an expression of princely policy – has stimulated the historian's imagination. There is nothing to suggest that the representations of kings at Richmond employed the 'three-quarter bust formula'; nothing to suggest that the likeness of Henry VII was actually the focal point of two lines of wall portraits all paying him 'homage'; nothing to suggest that the whole design culminated in a royal throne; and nothing to suggest that such a throne was itself the focal point for a display of tapestries. In any case, since the parliamentary surveys tell us that the hall was 'adorned with eleven statues, in the sides thereof' (Colvin 1963–82: IV, 227), and since the word 'picture' was commonly used by contemporaries to indicate sculpted or moulded royal effigies, there is a strong likelihood that the 'pictures' were not painted portraits at all. None of this renders wholly nugatory the suggestion that the arrangement of the hall carried some political message. But, as far as we can tell, contemporary intentions were less precise and far less self-conscious than the modern reconstruction implies.[71]

Royal portraiture in the reign of Elizabeth I poses very different problems. Here there can be no doubt about the interest of the Queen herself and of her advisers in the style and quality of the portraits; no doubt about the existence of some kind of industry involved in their production and multiplication; and no doubt about the complexity of the imagery employed in some, at least, of these pictures.[72] What remain obscure are the underlying purposes of such images, their distribution and the attitudes of those who gazed upon them. At the very beginning of Elizabeth's reign there is a curious item of expenditure relating to the furnishing of the new customs house at Pembroke by Thomas Phaer, collector of tonnage and poundage in the port of Milford, who purchased four portraits — one of Henry VIII, one of Edward VI, one of Mary and one of Elizabeth. We do not know whether this was a personal whim of Phaer's, or whether such royal portraits were regarded as a standard adornment for customs houses, but they can hardly have been masterpieces, since he bought all four for one shilling (Lewis 1927: 330).[73] Perhaps it was the circulation of such pictures that led to the well-known draft proclamation of December 1563. This document, corrected by William Cecil himself, begins by stating that there is a natural desire on the part of all subjects 'both noble and mean' to procure a portrait of the Queen; that this desire has prompted all manner of artists to meet the demand 'in painting, graving, and printing'; but that the portraits thus far produced are so unfaithful that 'daily are heard complaints amongst her loving subjects'. These complaints are such that the Queen has been 'instantly and importunately sued unto by the body of the council and others of her nobility' not only that some special artist might be permitted to 'take the natural representation of her majesty', but also that it should be prohibited to 'draw, paint, grave or portray her majesty's personage or visage for a time until, by some perfect patron and example, the same may be by others followed'. The draft continues that the Queen, though reluctant to sit for her portrait, had been convinced by the 'continual requests of so many of her nobility and subjects' and has agreed to the appointment of 'some cunning person' whose work, when completed, would serve as a pattern to be followed by other well-reputed artists, 'hired by the head officers of the places where they shall dwell' (Hughes and Larkin 1964–9: II, 240–1).

This scheme was never officially promulgated, although something along these lines must have been developed in order to produce the number of portraits of Elizabeth which yet survive and to produce them according to distinguishable patterns. Moreover, the very existence of the draft proclamation suggests that somebody in high places was giving serious thought to the dissemination of copies of the royal likeness; and, since it is unlikely that quantities of 'mean' subjects really did complain daily about inferior portraiture, it becomes all the more interesting that the Council should have insisted that they were. The draft's initial assumption, that to possess a portrait of the Queen was a natural desire, is also interesting. Why was such a desire natural, and what purpose was to be served by satisfying it? Amongst various anti-papal papers collected by Cecil, there is a discourse by Clement Urmeston incorporating typical remarks on the significance of the royal head seal (British Library MS. Lansdowne 97, fols.148ff.). But there is nothing in the draft proclamation, or in any other source, to suggest that there was ever any intention to resuscitate Urmeston's talismanic plan for every householder to have a seal with the royal image.

The most likely reason for owning a royal portrait was as an expression, at an elementary level, of loyalty and enthusiasm: and Sir Roy Strong's suggestion – that the existence of medals showing Elizabeth I's head, cast in base metal and with a ring for suspension, testifies to 'an almost universal cult' of the Queen – is doubtful (Strong 1963: 31–2). We have no evidence concerning the number of such medals issued or the extent to which they were carried, and no way of knowing whether their owners ever pondered the nature of talismanic power and divine kingship. *Amulet* is a word much favoured by culture historians, and it has a much grander sound than *good-luck-charm*: but the latter is surely closer to the spirit in which such medals might have been regarded by ordinary folk if they did, indeed, carry them. In general, surviving medals do not convey an impression that Tudor England was receptive to the more lofty claims of Renaissance numismatists. Rather they suggest much the same sort of *ad hoc* randomness encountered elsewhere in Tudor image-making. Nothing survives for Henry Tudor, and very little for his son, though there is a portrait medal of about 1524 showing on the reverse a Tudor rose and the inscription 'ODOR EIUS VT LIBANI', likening the odour to that of the cedars of Lebanon. There is also a portrait medal of Anne Boleyn and one of Thomas Cromwell, commemorating his election to the Order of the Garter and, in the latter case, an earl's coronet is attached to the rim to enable the medal to be worn by suspension. Similarly, in the reign of Elizabeth – in addition to a number of medals celebrating triumphs such as the defeat of the Armada, and joyous events such as Elizabeth's recovery from smallpox in 1572 – various of the Queen's subjects employed noted artists to commemorate their own achievements in portrait medals, and at least one of these (for William Herbert, Earl of Pembroke, in 1562) was provided with a ring for suspension. Cromwell later became a Protestant hero and Herbert was a distinguished public figure: but no one has suggested that either of them inspired a cult. The medal in Tudor England was no merely commonplace token. Nor was it a royal prerogative, a talisman, or an icon.[74]

The coinage, on the other hand, *was* a royal prerogative. Control of its design, minting and distribution was always jealously guarded and was the subject of repeated statutes, proclamations and grants of privilege throughout the Tudor period. Henry VII gave these matters close personal attention, and it is noteworthy that his measures to reform the coinage in 1504 constitute the only administrative matter to receive a chapter all to itself, 'Justa monetae reformatio', in Bernardus Andreas's *Annales* (Gairdner 1858: 81–2). The coinage was, beyond comparison, the most far-reaching medium for the display of royal portraiture, dynastic badges and political epigraphy; and it remains the most striking evidence of their limited efficacy. There is no reason to suppose that sixteenth-century folk contemplated the coins in their purses more assiduously than we do. The handling of coins has always been an everyday occurrence: yet how many people are able – or would have been able – accurately to record from memory their portraits, badges and inscriptions? In any case, such descriptive power would depend on superficial keenness of observation. At what level of cultivated intelligence would an understanding of the meaning of the iconography and epigraphy have commenced? A test case in this respect is the design and issue of Henry VII's sovereign in 1489 (see Fig. 25). This was a heavy gold coin based on the model of several continental

Fig. 25.   Gold Sovereign coin of Henry VII (Hocking no.791).

issues and notably the *real d'or* used by Maximilian in the Low Countries from 1487.

The similarity between the design of the sovereign and *real*, each with an enthroned figure of a monarch on the obverse and a shield of arms on the reverse, together with their identical weight, has been interpreted by numismatists as a deliberate attempt by Henry VII to align English and continental practice. It was, in the words of C. E. Challis, in his authoritative study of the Tudor coinage, 'a small yet brilliant addition to the trappings of the new dynasty' (Challis 1978: 47–51). Furthermore, on this coin, Henry abandoned the traditional open crown of the English kings and adopted the arched, imperial crown closed over the head and surmounted with a cross – a form also used on the second issue of his groat and half-groat (see Fig. 26). This, it has been argued, *may* have had implications for English claims to imperial dominion which were later, in the reign of Henry VIII, associated with the wearing of the appropriate crown (Grierson 1964: 118–34). My point is not whether this notion is historically correct – something which, unless fresh evidence is forthcoming, cannot be proved – but whether those rare contemporaries of Henry VII wealthy enough to handle sovereigns, and those many folk who regularly handled the groat or half-groat, ever noticed the shape of the crown, let alone understood its momentous message as reconstructed by modern scholarship. Such contemporary attitudes are also beyond proof, but they are not beyond the exercise of common sense and reasonable conjecture.

Fig. 26. Groat and half-groat coins of Henry VII's second issue (Hocking nos.800, 802).

The impact of printing

The role of printing in Tudor image-making is another issue where modern preconceptions are a hindrance rather than a help. The potential power of the press, both in terms of providing sophisticated visual propaganda and disseminating it, seems so obvious to us that we readily assume that it was consistently and effectively utilized in Tudor England to enhance people's perception of the dynasty. Certainly, control of printing, by licensing, censorship and prosecution, was vigorously if fitfully maintained from the time of Thomas Cromwell; writers were commissioned to advance arguments favourable to royal policies and other authors offered apologetics spontaneously and without official encouragement. Nevertheless, compared with the range and volume of political pamphleteering issuing from the continental presses throughout the sixteenth century, English production remained insignificant, especially with regard to prints, woodcuts and engravings.

The extent of England's backwardness is especially striking in the literature relating to royal spectacle and ceremony. Of all the Tudor coronations, funerals, civic entries and court festivals, only a tiny proportion were commemorated by printed editions, and those few were primitive, clumsy brochures, devoid of style and quality. In France, by contrast, almost every royal occasion from the late fifteenth century onward was marked by printed accounts of the ceremonies and spectacle – births, deaths, marriages, coronations, entries, funerals, tournaments, festivals – sometimes several for each event, and often illustrated with high-quality woodcuts. It may be asked, of course, where did all this get the Valois monarchy? What good did it do them? But the significance of such commemorative literature is not whether it really achieved anything as propaganda but rather that it demonstrates the extent of royal interest and taste. The positive political value of publicity via the printing press in the sixteenth century may have been very limited. What is noteworthy is that, for a dynasty allegedly concerned with image-making, with winning the support and admiration of its subjects, and with creating a cult of monarchy, none of the Tudors – not even Elizabeth – seems to have tried very hard.[75]

In the wider fields of sixteenth-century controversy, the production of the English presses is no more able to bear comparison with, for example, the great polemical outpourings of the German reformation or the French wars of religion. However, wonders of ingenuity are possible even with limited material and John Foxe's *Actes and Monuments* – Tudor England's only significant combination of polemical text and illustrations – has afforded ample scope. Foxe's theories of universal history, his numerological *schema*, and his apocalypticism, have been the delight of the learned from his own to the present day; but recent scholarship – its appetite for exegesis unappeased by the three million (or more) words heaped up in the *Actes and Monuments* — has sought further nutriment from the woodcuts. It has been cogently maintained that the historical outline of Foxe's thesis can be traced through some of these illustrations and that, because it was governmental policy to make the volume available in most churches, those illustrations would have become familiar to the Elizabethan public. Far less convincing is the assertion that the 'climax of the whole book' comes in the historiated letter *C* of the dedication, showing Queen Elizabeth seated on her throne which crushes the Pope (see Fig. 27). And should we regret that the fascination of Foxe's accounts of the martyrs' sufferings has drawn attention away from 'the fact that the politico-religious position which he propounds derives its sanction from the traditions, Christianized it is true, of the worldly empire of Rome' (Yates 1975: 43–4).

An approach of this kind, however much light it may throw on Renaissance erudition for a modern audience, fails to acknowledge the immense distance between what a writer or artist may have intended, and what an ordinary reader or viewer might have understood. We may readily accept that the illustration depicts Elizabeth as a second Constantine, and that it reverses a familiar pictorial tradition of the Papacy triumphing over the Empire. It is more difficult to visualize Tudor citizens clustered around their local copy of Foxe's work, scrutinizing the initial letter *C* of the dedication, and earnestly debating its historical and iconological message. And it is 'mpossible to believe

Fig. 27. Initial letter *C* and part of the text of the dedication of the 1577 edition of John Foxe, *Actes and Monuments*.

that these citizens felt that the letter *C* constituted the climax of their reading.

Another instance of this interpretative stumbling-block is encountered in John Norman King's recent (1989) examination of Tudor iconography, where he provides a learned exposition of the antecedents and significance of the non-martyrological illustrations in Foxe's work, and especially of the sequence of twelve anti-papal woodcuts, *The Proud Primacy of the Popes*, inserted by the printer, John Day, at the end of the 1570 edition. Again it cannot be denied that Foxe held very decided views on the history of the Christian Church, on the relative position occupied within that history by the Papacy and the English monarchy, and on the ways in which these ideas might be conveyed in images. But it is necessary for the modern reader of a sixteenth-century book to retain a sense of proportion, especially when — as in the historico-political illustrations in Foxe — much of the meaning is not immediately obvious and where scholarly exegesis may help to recover an original intention. For, paradoxically, the real difficulty is posed less by such intellectual conundrums than by areas where the appeal of a text is so obvious that the scholar scarcely pauses over them. Thus John King acknowledges only *en passant* that 'most of the woodcuts portray martyrdoms of Protestant saints' and that 'in the popular imagination' Foxe's book is remembered for the 'lurid images of the "roasting" of Sir John Oldcastle' and other violent scenes (King 1989: 134–5).

The inevitable impression given by such cursory acknowledgement is that the heart of the matter lies elsewhere — in the historical and iconological analogues which require elucidation — and the problem of giving due weight to the crude, the commonplace and the uncomplicated, has been skirted. Of the potential Tudor audience, that tiny minority who might have possessed the skill, perseverance and time to master the bewildering mixture of typefaces and layout and actually read the *Actes and Monuments*, would have found the strength of Foxe's polemic in the circumstantial detail and mighty documentation of his atrocity stories. For the illiterate majority, excitement and indignation would have been generated by the evocative woodcuts demonstrating the cruelties from which England had only recently been delivered (see Fig. 28). Such readers might sometimes have been disconcerted by encountering representations of one and the same gentleman being combusted under different names and at different dates, as was the case, for example, with James Bainham and Adam Wallace; Walter Mille and Kerby; Richard Bayfield, Thomas Benet and Peke; and, in one especially powerful woodcut, with John Bent and William Hunter (see Fig. 29). But, even allowing for such duplication, the pictures of executions still outnumber other illustrations in the text by about ten to one.

(a)

(b)

Fig. 28. Two typical execution scenes from Foxe:
(a) King, Debnam and Marsh in 1532;
(b) Rogers in 1555.

Fig. 29. Another scene from Foxe used to illustrate the execution of John Bent in 1532 and William Hunter in 1555.

Erudition, courtiership and conceitful thought

Common assumptions concerning both the migration and impact of symbols should be questioned very seriously. The context provided for us by academic detective work, however indispensable it may be, is necessarily highly selective and based upon a painstakingly accumulated repertoire of historical antecedents, literary analogues and iconological parallels; and such specialized knowledge would have been as far beyond the ken of ordinary people in the sixteenth century as it is in the twentieth. Many of the poets who stuffed their eulogies of

Elizabeth I with 'lillies/ and the dayntie Daffadillies/ With Roses damask, White and red, and fairest flower delice,/ With Cowslips of Jerusalem, and cloves of Paradice', were not so much ingenious and allusive as iconologically lazy. While to imagine that readers confronted with a phoenix or sieve, unhesitatingly fancied imperial renewal or chastity, is rather like imagining that ordinary folk have microscopes for eyeballs and perceive in a simple glass of water a reservoir teeming with strange organisms, or in a humble biscuit encounter a mountain of cavorting particles. There are people who do study life under a microscope, just as there were people equipped to decipher symbols. But it is unlikely that such iconographical skill was widespread in Tudor England; and, whatever justification there may be for teasing out hidden and obscure meanings, there is none for habitually conveying an impression that these were more important than the straightforward. When, for example, the English fleet and the weather combined to destroy the Spanish Armada in 1588, the designer of a medal struck at Middelburg simply decorated the obverse with a view of the rival fleets in action (Grueber 1904–11: plate X, no.16). Ships similarly appear in the background to the so-called 'Armada' portraits (Strong 1963: 74, nos.64, 65). And forty years later, the ships – on shield or banner – have become emblematic of Elizabeth I on the title-pages of books devoted to the defenders of Church and State in England (see Figs. 30 and 31).

On the other hand it is obvious that artistic and intellectual ingenuity *was* deployed in the closed circuit of clambering courtiership; and this raises another important issue. Granted that our own conception of 'propaganda', with its populist implications, is an anachronism for Tudor England: is it none the less possible that the techniques of political persuasion – and more particularly the manipulation of imagery – did function in the higher reaches of society where some degree of artistic and literary sophistication might reasonably be expected? If so, it would mean that the audience for such material coincided with the politically powerful minority clustered about the court; and this, in turn, would preserve the notion of 'propaganda' in a limited but more effective area. The notion is tempting: but again there remain the uncomfortable demands of common sense.

There certainly existed a cluster of Latin poeticules around the court of Henry VII who scribbled eulogies, in the manner of Vergil's fourth *Eclogue*, concerning the return of the Golden Age; just as there existed cartloads of emblematic flowers, an energetic reworking of all the threadbare conventions of courtly love, adaptations of classical myth, and ingenious manipulation of Christian imagery, in ceaseless adulation of Elizabeth I. The material ranges from puerile and sycophantic doggerel to those massive obscurities of Spenser's *Faerie Queene*

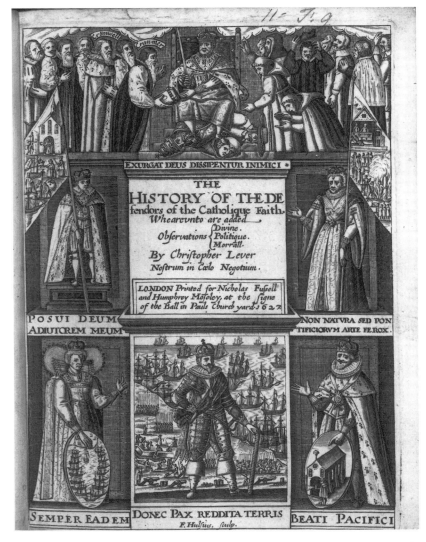

Fig. 30. Title page of Christopher Lever, *The History of the Defendors of the Catholique Faith* (1627).

which now fuel an industry of numerologists, allegorists, emblematologists, feminists and hermeneutists. But if all this were 'propaganda', who was supposed to be the manipulator and who the manipulated? Or, to beg an even more fashionable question, if this did amount to a 'Queen cult' what was it supposed to achieve? Could this kind of

Fig. 31. Title page of George Carleton, *A Thankfull Remembrance of God's Mercie* (1624).

exaggerated praise ever win over a disaffected suitor; could it stop any noble from harbouring critical thoughts about governmental decisions; or could it convince some aristocrat that he should support an issue on which he had hitherto been uncommitted or which was against his interests? The whole panoply of panegyric was aimed upward to please the monarch, not downward to persuade doubting courtiers of the rectitude of the regime. The highly coloured imagery was the currency of aspiring authors, poets, artists and courtiers to buy attention. The Crown, on the other hand, dealt principally in favours and coercion.

We have, I believe, become both too sophisticated and too gullible. We treat the web-spinning subtleties of sixteenth-century scholars and the intricate flattery of courtiers alike with too much respect — indeed, nowadays it is scarcely permitted to regard even the most arrant toadyism as *mere flattery* — and it is inevitable that the quest for hidden connotations sometimes results in a species of erudite buffoonery. Scholars may debate the connotations of a flower as though it were some weighty matter of state; bury an innocent and conventional metaphor in the sepulchre of a portentous explication; or simply lose all sense of proportion. It has, for example, been argued that roses were associated with the Blessed Virgin and that this was especially true of the *rosa sine spina*. Lacking the thorns of original sin, this flower grew only in the garden of Eden, and that is why, in lyrics celebrating the Virgin, it was also known as the *flower of paradise*, 'signifying the prelapsarian ideal of sinless desire and immaculacy of conception that was made flesh only in the Virgin Mary (the second Eve)'. It was in this guise, it is alleged, that Spenser alludes to the flower of Paradise, celebrating England's own 'Eternal Virgin' (McClure and Wells 1990: 54—5). All of this may be iconologically verifiable: but it must be pointed out that the crowned double rose, accompanied by the legend *RVTILANS ROSA SINE SPINA*, appeared on the crown and half-crown of Henry VIII's second issue of coinage in 1526 (see Fig. 32), and that he was celebrated as the rose without thorn on several coins of his later issues (Hocking 1906: I, nos.823—4, 832—4, 838—9, 852—5, 860, 865, 871). Scholarly ingenuity can accomplish much: but to identify Henry VIII with prelapsarian ideals of sinless desire, or with the Virgin Mary, presents formidable difficulties.

Elizabeth's purity was less equivocal. Her chastity was a boon to poets, mythographers and modern exegetes. In particular, much has been written about the five-petalled white rose or eglantine which was

Fig. 32.   Crown coin of Henry VIII (Hocking no.823).

not only an emblem of her virginity but could be combined with the union rose, or even replace it, to bring the Tudor mission neatly up to date. This is how the flower was used in the decoration of the manuscript *Hymne* presented to the Queen by Georges de la Mothe, by William Rogers in his engraving of Elizabeth as *Rosa Electa*, and by Henry Lyte in the frontispiece to his *Light of Britayne* (Strong 1977: 68−71). Doubts creep in, however, with the most specific of all references to Elizabeth as the eglantine. It occurs in the final stanza of *Eglantyne of Meryfleur* by Sir Arthur Gorges, a versifying gentleman pensioner whom modern scholarship has misguidedly rescued from oblivion.

> Then hyr hye lynage he rynges
>   deryved from the Dardane kynges
> discendinge to the Conqueringe lyne
>   wheare stately stryff he doothe recyte
> betweene the redd rose and the whyte
>   appeasde in thys brave Eglantyne.
>   (Gorges, ed. Sandison 1953: 125)

Both the Tudor and Elizabethan significance of the imagery are obvious. Yet the fact remains that Gorges had originally drafted the poem for his wife, and only later twisted it into a tribute to the Queen; and, while this does not alter the meaning of the literary figure, it does suggest a certain courtly opportunism on Gorges's part. If compliments addressed to the Queen were largely matters of form, venal, or part of a courtly game, then the term *Cult* − which implies worship, devotion and sincerity − is too highly coloured and tendentious.

The great disparity between outward show and inner meaning is laid bare in the courtly career of Robert Devereux, Earl of Essex. The languid, rose-entwined gentleman of Hilliard's miniature, the enigmatic jouster in the Accession Day Tilts, the mediocre sonneteer, eulogist and courtly lover of Elizabeth − Essex was at the centre of the 'Queen Cult' (Strong 1977: 56−83). But what did it all add up to beyond heartless self-seeking and, eventually, petulance and treason when his ambitions were thwarted? That the pretence was politically purposive is obvious. All the more reason, then, to be suspicious of it and to be wary of any assumption that Essex's contemporaries were disposed to treat his courtly utterances with credulity. This noble lover, even at the nadir of his fortunes, was still penning sycophantic epistles to the withered object of his affections, while privately snarling that 'she being now an old woman, is no less crooked in mind than in body' (Camden 1635: 536).

Erudition and conceitful thought merit study. What they do not merit is our confidence that they were sincere, that they were politically effective, and that they were necessarily taken seriously by contemporaries. Even before the Armada opened the floodgates of eulogy, one egregious rhymer and alliterator, Maurice Kyffin — in his wildly enthusiastic celebration of Elizabeth's 'Holyday', *The Blessednes of Brytaine* (1587) — contrived an effective sneer at his fellow flatterers.

> What should I Nymphs, or Goddeses Recount?
> Or AEgypt Queenes, or Romane Ladies name?
> Sith as Supreme, our Sov'raigne dooth surmount,
> In choice of Good, the cheefe of all those same?
>   For to compare the great, with simple small.
>   Is thereby, not to praise the Best at all.

Kyffin's marginal gloss on his own classical abstinence is devastating and should be better known. 'Besides that such manner of Reciting strange and Hethenish names were here altogether inconvenient', he declares, 'the author doth also of very purpose, somewhat shun that beaten high way, to fil paper with pestring Names of fained Gods, Goddesses, Nymphs, Persians, Grecians, Romans, &c. Being a thing of some sometimes used, too too much, and to litle effect.' (Hazlitt 1875: I, Item. xxix.)

Images which require pages of exegesis before they yield up their meaning do not make for successful propaganda. Easily recognized badges, memorable slogans, and simple messages are what people respond to and in this respect the sixteenth century scarcely differed from the twentieth. This is why, when we think of Tudor dynastic imagery, it is not abstruse imperial symbolism and arcane emblematics which come most readily to mind but rather the heraldic badges adopted by Henry VII at the very outset of his reign — dragons, greyhounds, portcullises and roses — and consistently used by all his successors in a pragmatic and thoroughly traditional manner. There is little evidence to support the view that the English monarchy employed a propaganda machine other than sporadically, and the notion that there was a carefully-thought-out systematic sales promotion of recondite imagery to the nation at large is a wholly modern, academic invention.

NOTES

1. For examples of the discussion of prodigality and liberality within the tradition *De regimine principum*, see Gilbert 1938: 84–97.
2. For Renaissance theories concerning imagery, see Gombrich 1972. On earlier, related theories of astrological images, see the early volumes of Thorndike 1923–58, especially on Neoplatonism and its relations to astrology and theurgy.
3. On the 'Idols of the Mind', see Aston 1988: 452–66.
4. Compare Pecock with Leonardo da Vinci's summary of the relative descriptive power of word and image. Alongside his illustration of the heart, in his *Quaderni d'Anatomia*, Leonardo wrote: 'Do not busy yourself in making enter by the ears things which have to do with the eyes, for in this you will be far surpassed by the painter. How in words can you describe this heart without filling a whole book. Yet the more you write concerning it the more you will confuse the mind of the hearer.' See Keele 1954.
5. This attitude was popularized in the *Catechism* (1570) by Alexander Nowell (ed. Corrie 1853). In Corrie's edition, 123–4, the scholar condemns praying to 'portraitures and images', falling down before them, and making signs of honour to them. We must neither worship God in images, nor worship images in honour of God: 'Otherwise the lawful use of making portraitures and of painting is not forbidden'.
6. Compare this condemnation of the ambitions stirred by secular imagery with a defence of precisely the same effects (and some of the same examples) as achieved by heraldic display, in Ferne 1586: 26. Ferne, too, discusses the power of examples on human action and declares that the very name of *Philip*, when sounded in Alexander's ears, 'incensed him to become a conquerour'; while Julius Caesar was inspired by a statue of Alexander, and Scipio and Fabius by the images of their parents. 'Then if it be so, that dumbe images of the noble: if tables painted with the heroicall

gestes of such as were straungers in bloud have not a little moved the posteritie to the attempting of like vertues and semblable exploites? Much more shall the worthy merites of the auncestor, figured out in the secret emblemes or sacred sculptures of the coat-armour, stirre up the sonne, to imitate the same vertues whereby his auncestor obteyned to with them.'

7. Display of royal arms in churches has been the subject of much disparate local research: but there is no general work to replace the regrettably slight Cautley 1934.

8. The main evidence that there was an industry manufacturing portraits of Elizabeth I is the draft proclamation of December 1563 (see pages 116−7). On the production of these pictures, see Strong 1963: 5−12.

9. On the general history of touching, see Bloch trs. Anderson 1973. On the English ceremonial, see Crawfurd 1911; and, on the numismatic aspect, Farquhar 1922.

10. Crawfurd 1911: 52−6, reproduces the Office of Henry VII.

11. For the Elizabethan Office of Healing, as set out by Tooker, see Crawfurd 1911: 72−3.

12. On Scot's scepticism, see Anglo 1977: 106−39.

13. A resumé of Urmeston's career is in Bindoff 1944−5: 64−73. For his work as revels artist and controversialist, see Anglo 1969: 164−7, 213, 231, 264−5. For remarks on his economic and social writings see Elton 1973: 69−70, 112−13: though these miss the point by assuming that Urmeston's cosmological ideas were merely a garnish rather than the basis for his commonweal notions.

14. A few of Urmeston's manuscript treatises were published by Pauli 1878: 15−77, whence two were reprinted in Tawney and Power 1924: III, 90−129.

15. Compare Urmeston's *Order of a Comen Welth*, Pauli 1878: 52−4.

16. Compare the *Order of a Comen Welth*, Pauli 1878: 52.

17. Compare the *Treatise concerning the Staple* in Pauli 1878: 15−43, especially at p.25.

18. Urmeston derives this figure from the Bible: I.Samuel ix.2; and I.Samuel x.23.

19. On solar imagery, see L'Orange 1953.

20. There is a tract by Urmeston among anti-papal papers collected by Sir William Cecil, Lord Burleigh (British Library MS. Lansdowne 97, fols.148ff.; calendared in Brewer 1862−1932: V, no.1501.

21. On Henry Tudor's rights to the throne and their assertion, see Pickthorn 1934: I, 1−27; Chrimes 1936: 32−4.

22. It is generally assumed that the heralds invented their own termin-

ology: but it has been argued that they largely derived it from the technical language of medieval artists and craftsmen (Brault 1972: 5).

23. On the heralds' involvement with state ritual, see Trexler 1978. Trexler is primarily concerned with Italy: but his general observations are pertinent.

24. On the 1511 roll, at the College of Arms, see Anglo 1968. On the 1512 roll (Trinity College Cambridge MS. 0.3.59), see Wagner and Sainty 1967: 128, 142−50, plates XVII−XX.

25. On illustrations of the coronation of Elizabeth of York, see Leland 1770: IV, 219, 223. Pictures of the Knights of the Bath are in *Writhe's Garter Book*, a manuscript belonging to the Duke of Buccleuch (Wagner 1950: 122−4; and Wagner 1967: 138, plates X−XII).

26. Drawings of the procession at the baptism of Edward VI are in College of Arms MS. M.6., fols.77^v−82^v. Similar drawings for the funeral of Anne of Cleves are on a paper roll now in the Bromhead Collection of the University of London Library, Senate House. Sketches of the coronation procession of Elizabeth I are in College of Arms MS. M.6, fols.35−48; and another version is in the British Library MS. Egerton 3320. Two folios of the Elizabeth I procession in MS. M.6. are reproduced in the catalogue of the *Herald's Commemorative Exhibition* 1936: plate XII. The Egerton MS. is discussed and reproduced by Collins 1953: 880−3.

27. Mostyn MS. 158, National Library of Wales, ed. Jones 1960: 311−37. The passage cited is at fol.424^v of the manuscript, and I must thank Prys Morgan of the University College of Swansea for providing an English translation of the section relating to Henry VIII's palace, pavilions and theatre.

28. On Henry VIII's palace at the Field of Cloth of Gold, see Anglo 1966: 289−96; Russell 1969: 32−46.

29. On the Calais theatre, see Anglo 1969: 159−63; Hosley 1979: 60−79; Orrell 1988: 31−8.

30. For the pageantry and a discussion of the sources, see Anglo 1969: 186−202; Withington 1918: I, 174−9.

31. Despite the ubiquity of the portcullis, there is no satisfactory study of the badge. On the greyhound, see London 1956: 38−41; and London 1959: 139−63.

32. Nothing is known about the creation of this pursuivant, though his title occurs several times during the 1490s. See Godfrey, Wagner and London 1963: 203.

33. One other Tudor badge, the hawthorn bush and crown, must be mentioned although it is difficult to say much about it. That the

badge originated at Bosworth (with the finding of Richard III's crown in a hawthorn bush) is the *received* story. But *received* from where? So far, no sixteenth-century authority for the tale has been discovered; and even Bacon 1858, in his *History of the Reign of Henry VII* (1622) does not mention it. That the Tudors used the badge is clear. Why they used it is not. See Anglo 1960: note 3; Chrimes 1972: 49; Ross 1981: 225, note 52.

34.   On the use of badges to represent a relationship between a superior and his dependants, and on the way in which a royal servant could transfer these 'emblems of dependence from his person to his house', as a public declaration of political allegiance, see Starkey 1982: 154–5.

35.   Kipling 1981: 140, note 63; Kipling 1977: 36–40, 42–3; Collins 1955: 279–81; Lightbown 1978: 78–82. For examples of *Tudorization*, see British Library MSS. Royal 1.C.viii; 15.D.iv; 17.F.v; 19.B.xvi; 19.C.vi; 20.E.i–vi. Royal MS.19.Axxii originally belonged to Richard de Wydeville, first Earl Rivers (d. 1469) whose mark of ownership at fol.31ᵛ has been erased, as have the inscriptions on scrolls in the borders, while a red rose and the arms of England, supported by red dragon and white greyhound have been introduced. Compare the *Yorkification* of Royal MS.15.D.i, a volume executed in Bruges in 1470 for a patron whose name has been erased and replaced by 'Edouard le quart'. The borders, too, have been altered, with the Garter and Yorkist badges introduced into the illumination.

36.   See Madden 1842: 318–47; Wright 1859; Furnivall 1866, 1903. There is a substantial literature on political prophecy but not, I believe, any study of its specifically heraldic aspect.

37.   Act 33 Henry VIII, Chapter XIV, *Touching Prophesies uppon Declaracion of Names Armes Badges & c*, printed in *Statutes of the Realm* 1817: III, 850. Apropos heraldic auguries, there was a tradition current in the seventeenth century concerning Henry VIII and Rhys ap Gruffudd who was executed in 1531. Rhys's arms featured three ravens; and the story, reported by Henry Rice, explains that the King was out hawking one day when his falcon – 'being seized of a fowle' – was disturbed by a raven and lost the quarry. Some mischief-maker whispered in Henry's ear, saying 'Sir, you see how peremptorie this raven is growne, and therefore it is time to pull him down, therefore to secure your majestie, and to prevent his insolencies'. If the tale were true, then it would reveal much about Henry's credulity. But even if mere hearsay, it is indicative of popular regard for heraldic portents. On this episode, see Williams 1903: especially p.51; and *Cambrian Register* 1799: 274–5. I must thank my friend Rhys Robinson for

bringing this story to my attention.

38. Pickthorn 1934: II, 531. In William Thomas's defence of Henry VIII's policies (1553), the case against Surrey is based on his arrogation of the royal arms, 'and one picture especially, in the which he had painted himself with the crown on his right hand and the King on his left hand' (Thomas, ed. Froude 1861: 72–4).

39. This chapter is based upon my article (Anglo 1961: 17–48). I have expanded the argument: but fuller documentation and an appendix of manuscript pedigrees may be found in the original version. For Yorkist material, see Allen 1979: 171–92.

40. Much work has recently been done on the Galfridian manuscripts (Crick 1989): but Tatlock 1950 is still useful. On the reception of Geoffrey's history, see Kendrick 1950.

41. Compare the concentration on the Yorkist descent at Elizabeth I's funeral: see above, Chapter Five, page 103. For sources on Tudor civic pageantry, see Anglo 1969; McGee and Meagher 1981, 1982.

42. The sources for much subsequent misinterpretation are Millican 1932, and Greenlaw 1932. For a recent critical survey, see Dean 1987.

43. For differing approaches to the 1501 pageant series, see Anglo 1963; Kipling 1977. The latter has discovered interesting new material, corrects two serious misreadings and exposes other shortcomings in the former. Kipling's recent edition (1990) of College of Arms MS. 1st M.13, fols.27–74^v gives further valuable detail. Yet, I feel that he allows far too much weight to Jean Molinet as a source for the pageantry while overlooking significant discrepancies, and too little weight to the pageant speeches themselves and, consequently, to the importance of Gregory the Great's *Moralia* as a source for their ideas. I still cannot see that this royal entry was much concerned with King Arthur.

44. There is a considerable body of material on Henry VI's miracles and proposed canonization in manuscript, edited documents, articles and miscellaneous volumes: but now see Grosjean 1935 who collects, prints and annotates (either entire or in large part) every relevant source.

45. For Thomas of Lancaster, see the article by W.E. Rhodes in the *Dictionary of National Biography* and the references cited therein.

46. On the other hand, one should note the letters from Alexander VI relating to Henry VII's plan to build a new chantry and hospital at Windsor in which it was proposed that the King should be buried and where it was intended to erect a shrine over the relics of Henry VI. In other words, there was doubt concerning

the removal of the body from Windsor (Grosjean 1935: 178−9).

47. There was nothing in Henry VI's will to indicate where he wished to be buried. The will merely provided money 'for to doo and satisfie myn exequyes memorials and alle thynges behouefull aboute my sepulture in honourable wise' (Grosjean 1935: 184−94).

48. The complete manuscript is in Grosjean 1935. Selections were published by Knox and Leslie 1923, who argued (pp.21−8) the case for the revision in Henry VIII's reign. Grosjean largely agrees but suggests (p.100) that there may have been an earlier interruption caused by the death of members of the original commission, and that there could have been a new attempt to examine the miracles after 1504.

49. The relevant passage in Henry VII's will states: 'we, by the grace of God, propose right shortely to translate into the same, the bodie and reliquies of our Vncle of blissid memorie King Henry the VIth' (Grosjean 1935: 218). Evidence that the body was never translated to Westminster was provided by the discovery of his remains at Windsor (Hope 1910−11: 533−42).

50. On the Tudors and King's College Chapel, see Woodman 1986; 134−215; Colvin 1963−82: III.i, 187−95.

51. For the poems cited here, and for other examples, see Madden 1842: 334−7; Furnivall 1866: xlvii, 1−4; Evans 1915: 8.

52. Edward V used the fifth, that is the last, seal of Edward IV which was itself based on the fourth; while Richard III used Edward IV's third seal which also included roses in the design (Birch 1887−1900: I, nos.318−23). The coinage of these two kings similarly featured the rose with or without the sun (Hocking 1906: I, nos. 778−81, 784, 786).

53. On these Yorkist seals, see Birch 1887−1900: nos. 12,676−9, 12,706. On the vestments of the Black Prince, John of Gaunt and Henry V, see Nichols 1780: 72, 149, 415. On the Tudor version of Henry V's banners, see De Walden 1904: 64, 70. More generally on the rose as a pre-Tudor royal badge, see London 1956: 32.

54. See Hales and Furnivall 1868: III, 189−94. The editors suggest (pp.187−8) that the poem was probably written in its original form during the reign of Henry VII and prior to the execution of Sir William Stanley in 1495.

55. Seals are notoriously difficult to reproduce clearly. The plates in Wyon and Wyon 1887 are about as good as is possible with photo-reproduction: but I have chosen to use the engravings in Sanford 1677, which show more detail than can be conveyed in a photograph.

56. For discussion of these York pageants, see Meagher 1968; Anglo 1969: 22−8; McGee 1989. For sources, see McGee and Meagher 1982: 35−6.
57. The sources for the London entry of Elizabeth I in 1559 are listed in McGee and Meagher 1981: 58−62.
58. The verses for Windsor and Oxford are, respectively, British Library MSS. Royal 12.A.xxx and xlvii. Both sets of verse are printed in Nichols 1788, I.
59. Fulke Greville's curious metaphor appears in his *Caelica*, Sonnet 82 (ed. Ellis-Fermor 1936: 103).
60. On English coronations, see Planché 1838; Legg 1901; Jones 1902; Murray 1936; Schramm 1937.
61. For the reference to Prince Arthur (Public Record Office MS. LC.2/1, fol.17); to Henry VIII (Wall 1891: 386); to Anne of Cleves (Bentley 1833: 304); and for Mary (Leland 1770: V, 315).
62. I am grateful to my friend Peter Begent for drawing my attention to Nicholas Charles's manuscript.
63. *This sermon folowynge was compyled and sayd in the Cathedrall chyrche of saynt Poule the body beynge present of the moost famouse Kynge Henry the .vii. the .x. daye of May, m.ccccc.ix.* This has been reprinted in Mayor 1876.
64. On English royal funerals and cognate material, see Machyn 1848; Wall 1891; Hope, 1906−7; Fritz 1981; Llewellyn 1990. Manuscript sources are rich − but especially noteworthy for Tudor funerals are British Library MSS. Egerton 2642, Additional 35,324 and Additional 45,131; Public Record Office MS. LC2/1.
65. On the funeral effigy of Richard Duke of York, see British Library MS. Egerton 2642, fol.191. There is another version of Richard's funeral in British Library MS. Harleian 48, fols.78−91. See also Armstrong 1983: 139.
66. The comment on the outmoded nature of the bishop's funeral effigy is in British Library MS. Egerton 2642, fol.195. On Gardiner's funeral, see Machyn 1848; 101.
67. An itinerary of Henry VII is given in Temperley 1917: 411−19. The peregrinations of Henry VIII have to be excavated from Brewer *et al.* 1862−1932. The most convenient outline of Elizabeth's movements is Chambers 1923: IV, 75−116.
68. On Tudor pageantry in general, see Withington 1918: I, 157−221; Anglo 1969; Bergeron 1970; McGee and Meagher 1981, 1982.
69. For an account of such theories and their intellectual background, see Yates 1947.
70. For examples of the canopy, see Guenée and Lehoux 1968:

13–21; Bryant 1986; 101–4; Legg 1901: 100, 108, 122, 129; Leland 1770: IV, 221.

71. Gordon Kipling has corrected his earlier misconstruction of the word 'pictures' as paintings; but he has not revised the interpretation which was based upon it (Kipling 1990: 160).

72. The fullest, and by far the most influential, studies of Elizabethan portraiture are Strong 1963 and 1977.

73. I must thank my friend Rhys Robinson for this reference. On Phayre, see Robinson 1972.

74. Tudor medals are most conveniently studied in Hawkins 1885; and Grueber 1904–11.

75. To point the difference, both in quality and density of publication, between sixteenth-century England and France in these matters, it is sufficient to compare de Worde 1533 and Tottel 1559 with the printed accounts of the entries of Henry II into Lyon (1548), Paris (1549) and Rouen (1550). For a still useful list of contemporary published accounts of French royal entries, see Kernodle 1944; and for full bibliographical information on the official publications relating to French tournaments, coronations and funerals, see Saffroy 1968–79.

BIBLIOGRAPHY

Printed sources cited in text and notes

Unless otherwise stated all books are published in London.

Allen, A 1979: 'Yorkist propaganda: pedigree, prophecy and the "British History" in the reign of Edward IV.' In: *Patronage, Pedigree and Power in Later Medieval England*, ed. C Ross, Gloucester

Anglo, S 1960: 'The foundation of the Tudor Dynasty: the coronation and marriage of Henry VII.' *The Guildhall Miscellany* II(i), 1−9

Anglo, S 1961: 'The *British History* in early Tudor propaganda.' *Bulletin of the John Rylands Library*, XLIV, 17−48

Anglo, S 1963: 'The London pageants for the reception of Katharine of Aragon: November 1501.' *Journal of the Warburg and Courtauld Institutes*, XXVI, 53−89

Anglo, S 1966: 'The Hampton Court painting of the Field of Cloth of Gold.' *The Antiquaries Journal*, XLVI, 287−307

Anglo, S 1968: *The Great Tournament Roll of Westminster*, Oxford

Anglo, S 1969: *Spectacle, Pageantry and Early Tudor Policy*, Oxford

Anglo, S (ed.) 1977: *The Damned Art. Essays in the Literature of Witchcraft*

Anglo, S 1990: 'Humanism and the Court Arts.' In: *The Impact of Humanism on Western Europe*, eds. A Goodman and A Mackay, 66−98

Arber, E (ed.) 1901: *Dunbar Anthology*

Armstrong, CAJ 1983: 'The inauguration ceremonies of the Yorkist kings and their title to the throne.' In: *England, France and Burgundy in the Fifteenth Century*. First published in *Transactions of the Royal Historical Society*, 4th series V, 1948, 51−73

Aston, M 1988: *England's Iconoclasts*, Oxford

Bacon, F 1858: *History of the Reign of King Henry VII*, ed. J Spedding in the *Works of Francis Bacon*, VI

Becon, T 1844: *The Catechism*, ed. J Ayre, Cambridge

Bémont, C 1930: *Simon de Montfort, Earl of Leicester: 1208−1265*, new edn. trs. EF Jacob, Oxford

Bentley, S 1833: *Excerpta Historica*

Bergenroth, GA, de Gayangos, P and Hume, MA 1862–1916: *Calendar of State Papers (Spanish)*

Bergeron DM 1970: *English Civic Pageantry 1558–1642*

Bilson, T 1585: *The True Difference between Christian Subjection and Unchristian Rebellion*, Oxford

Bindoff, ST 1944–5: 'Clement Armstrong and his Treatises of the Commonweal.' *Economic History Review*, XIV, 64–73

Birch, WdeG 1887–1900: *British Museum. Catalogue of Seals*

Bloch, M 1973: *The Royal Touch. Sacred Monarchy and Scrofula in England and France*, trs. JE Anderson

Brault, GJ 1972: *Early Blazon*, Oxford

Brewer, JS, Gairdner, J and Brodie, RH 1862–1932: *Letters and Papers, Foreign and Domestic of the Reign of Henry VIII*

Bruce, J 1838: ed. *Historie of the Arivall of Edward IV in England and the Finall Recoverye of his Kingdomes from Henry VI. AD. MCCCCLXXI*

Bryant, LM 1986: *The King and the City in the Parisian Royal Entry Ceremony: Politics, Ritual, and Art in the Renaissance*, Geneva

Calfhill, J 1565: *An Answer to John Martiall's Treatise of the Cross*, ed. R Gibbings, Cambridge 1846

Cambrian Register 1799

Camden, W 1635: *Annals, or, the Historie of the Most Renowned and Victorious Princesse Elizabeth, Late Queen of England*, 3rd edn

Carleton, G 1624: *A Thankful Remembrance of Gods Mercie*

Catalogue of the Heralds' Commemorative Exhibition, 1484–1934, 1936, repr. 1970

Cautley, HM 1934: *Royal Arms and Commandments in Our Churches*, Ipswich

Challis, CE 1978: *The Tudor Coinage*, Manchester

Chambers, EK 1923: *The Elizabethan Stage*, Oxford

Chrimes, SB 1936: *English Constitutional Ideas in the Fifteenth Century*

Chrimes, SB 1972: *Henry VII*

Christmas, H (ed.) 1849: *The examinacyon of William Thorpe* in *Select Works of John Bale* Cambridge

Collins, AJ 1953: 'The ordering of the coronation of Elizabeth I from a contemporary official manuscript.' *The Illustrated London News*, 30 May 1953, 880–3

Collins, AJ 1955: *Jewels and Plate of Queen Elizabeth I. The Inventory of 1574*

Colvin, HM 1963–82: *History of the King's Works*

Cranmer, T 1846: *Miscellaneous Writings and Letters*, ed. JE Cox, Cambridge

Crawfurd, R 1911: *The King's Evil*, Oxford

Crick, JC 1989: *The Historia Regum Britannie of Geoffrey of Monmouth.*

A Summary Catalogue of Manuscripts, Woodbridge

Dean, C 1987: *Arthur of England. English Attitudes to King Arthur and the Knights of the Round Table in the Middle Ages and Renaissance*, Toronto

Dennys, R 1975: *The Heraldic Imagination*

De Walden, H 1904: *Banners, Standards and Badges*

Dictionary of National Biography 1885–1900: eds. L Stephen and S Lee, Cambridge

Ellis, H 1814: 'Devices formerly borne as Badges of Cognizance by the House of York.' *Archaeologia*, XVII, 226–7

Elton, GR 1973: *Reform and Renewal. Thomas Cromwell and the Common Weal*, Cambridge

Elyot, J 1883: *The Boke named the Governour*, ed. HHS Croft

Evans, HT 1915: *Wales and the Wars of the Roses*, Cambridge

Farquhar, H 1922: *Royal Charities: Angels and Touchpieces for the King's Evil*

Ferne, J 1586: *The Blazon of Gentrie*

Fortescue, J 1869: *De titulo Edwardi comitis Marchie*. In: *The Works of Sir John Fortescue*, ed. Lord Clermont

Fortescue, J 1885: *The Governance of England*, ed. C Plummer, Oxford

Foxe, J 1837–41: *Acts and Monuments*, eds. SR Cattley and G Townsend

Fritz, PS 1981: 'From "Public" to "Private": the Royal Funerals in England, 1500–1830.' In: *Mirrors of Mortality. Studies in the Social History of Death*, ed. J Whaley

Fulman, W (ed.) 1684: *Historiae Croylandensis continuatio*. In: *Rerum Anglicarum scriptores*, Oxford

Furnivall, FJ (ed.) 1868–72: *Ballads from Manuscripts*

Furnivall, FJ (ed.) 1866 and 1903: *Political, Religious and Love Poems*

Gairdner, J (ed.) 1858: *Memorials of King Henry VII*

Gardiner, S 1933: *The Letters*, ed. JA Muller, Cambridge

Giffin, ME 1941: 'Cadwalader, Arthur and Brutus in the Wigmore MS.' *Speculum*, XVI, 109–20

Gilbert, AH 1938: *Machiavelli's 'Prince' and its Forerunners*, Durham, N. Carolina

Godfrey, WH, Wagner, AR and London, HS 1963: *The College of Arms, Queen Victoria Street, being the Sixteenth and Final Monograph of the London Survey Committee*

Gombrich, EH 1972: *Symbolic Images. Studies in the Art of the Renaissance*

Gorges, A 1953: *The Poems of Sir Arthur Gorges*, ed. HE Sandison, Oxford

Grafton, R 1569: *Chronicle at Large*, ed. H Ellis 1809

Greenlaw, EA 1932: *Studies in Spenser's Historical Allegory*, Baltimore

Greville, F 1936: *Caelica*, ed. UM Ellis-Fermor

Grierson, P 1964: 'The origins of the English sovereign and the symbolism of the closed crown.' *British Numismatic Journal*, XXXIII, 118–34

Grindal, E 1571: *Injunctions*. In: *Remains of Edmund Grindal*, ed. W Nicholson, Cambridge, 1843

Grosjean, P 1935: *Henrici VI Angliae Regis Miracula Postuma ex codice Musei Britannici Regis 13.C.VIII*, Brussels

Grueber, HA 1904–11: *Medallic Illustrations of the History of Great Britain and Ireland*, repr. 1979

Guenée, B and Lehoux, F 1968: *Les entrées royales françaises de 1328 à 1515*, Paris

Guy, J 1986: 'Thomas Cromwell and the Intellectual Origins of the Henrician Reformation.' *Reassessing the Henrician Age*

Hales, JW and Furnivall, FW (eds.) 1868: *Bishop Percy's Manuscript*

Hall, E 1809: *The Union of the Two Noble and Illustre Famelies of Lancastre and Yorke*, ed. H Ellis

Hardyng, J 1812: *The Chronicle*, ed. H Ellis

Harpsfield, N 1878: ed. N Pocock, *A Treatise on the Pretended Divorce between Henry VIII and Catherine of Aragon*

Harris, MD (ed.) 1907–13: *Coventry Leet Book*

Hawkins, E 1885: *Medallic Illustrations of the History of Great Britain and Ireland to the Death of George II*

Hay, D 1952: *Polydore Vergil*, Oxford

Hazlitt, WC (ed.) 1875: *Fugitive Tracts Written in Verse*

Hinds, AB 1912: *Calendar of State Papers, Milan*

Hocking, WJ 1906: *Catalogue of the Coins, Tokens, Medals, Dies and Seals in the Museum of the Royal Mint*

Hooper, J 1842: *A Declaracion of christe and of his offyce* in *Early Writings of John Hooper*, ed. S Carr, Cambridge

Hope, WH St J 1906–7: 'On the Funeral Effigies of the Kings and Queens of England.' *Archaeologia*, LX, 517–70

Hope, WH St J 1910–11: 'The discovery of the remains of Henry VI in St George's Chapel, Windsor Castle.' *Archaeologia*, LXII, 533–42

Hosley, R 1979: 'The theatre and the tradition of playhouse design.' In: *The First Public Playhouse. The Theatre in Shoreditch 1576–1598*, ed. H Berry, Montreal,

Hughes, PL and Larkin, JF (eds.) 1964–9: *Tudor Royal Proclamations*, New Haven, Conn.

Jones, EJ 1943: *Medieval Heraldry. Some Fourteenth Century Heraldic Works*, Cardiff

Jones, T (ed.) 1960: 'Mostyn MS 158, National Library of Wales' in *Bulletin of the Board of Celtic Studies*, XVIII, 311–37

Jones, W 1902: *Crowns & Coronations. A History of Regalia*

Jones, WG 1917–18: 'Welsh nationalism and Henry Tudor.' *Transactions of the Honourable Society of Cymmrodorion*, 1–59

Kantorowicz, EH 1957: *The King's Two Bodies. A Study in Medieval Political Theology*, repr. 1981

Keele, K 1954: 'Leonardo da Vinci's Anatomical Drawings at Windsor', in *Studi Vinciani* II 76–85

Kendrick, TD 1950: *British Antiquity*

Kernodle, G 1944: *From Art to Theatre*, Chicago

King, JN 1989: *Tudor Royal Iconography. Literature and Art in an Age of Religious Crisis*, Princeton

Kipling, G 1977: *The Triumph of Honour. Burgundian Origins of the Elizabethan Renaissance*, Leiden

Kipling, G 1981: 'Henry VII and the origins of Tudor patronage.' In: *Patronage in the Renaissance*, eds. G Lytle and S Orgel, Princeton

Kipling, G (ed.) 1990: *The Receyt of the Ladie Kateryne*, Oxford

Klarwill, 1928: *Queen Elizabeth and Some Foreigners*

Knighton, H 1889: *Chronicon Henrici Knighton*, ed. J Rawson Lumby

Knox, R and Leslie, S 1923: *The Miracles of King Henry VI*, Cambridge

Kyffin, M 1587: *The Blessednes of Brytaine*, repr. in Hazlitt 1875

Laneham, R 1575: *A Letter: Whearin, part of the entertainment vntoo the Queenz Maiesty, at Killingworth Castl . . . is signified*

Legg, LGW 1901: *English Coronation Records*, Westminster

Leland, J 1770: *De Rebus Britannicis Collectanea*, ed. T Hearne

Lever, C 1627: *The Historie of the Defendors of the Catholique Faith*

Lethaby, WR 1925: *Westminster Abbey Re-examined*

Lewis, EA 1927: *The Welsh Port Books (1550–1603)*

Lhoyd, H 1584: *The Historie of Cambria*, ed. D Powel

Lightbown, RW 1978: *Secular Goldsmiths' Work in Medieval France: a History*

Llewellyn, N 1990: 'The royal body: monuments to the dead, for the living.' In: *Renaissance Bodies. The Human Figure in English Culture c. 1540–1660*, eds. L Gent and N. Llewellyn, 218–40, 275–82

London, HS 1956: *Royal Beasts*, East Knoyle

London, HS 1959: 'The greyhound as a royal beast.' *Archaeologia*, XCVII, 139–63

L'Orange, HP 1953: *Studies in the Iconography of Cosmic Kingship in the Ancient World*, Oslo

McClure, P and Wells, RH 1990: 'Elizabeth I as a second Virgin Mary.' *Renaissance Studies*, IV, 38–70

Machyn, H 1848: *The Diary*, ed. JG Nichols

McGee, CE 1989: 'Politics and platitudes: sources of civic pageantry, 1486.' *Renaissance Studies*, III, 29–34

McGee, CE and Meagher, JC 1981: 'Preliminary checklist of Tudor and Stuart entertainments: 1558–1603.' *Research Opportunities in Renaissance Drama*, XXIV, 51–155

McGee CE and Meagher, JC 1982: 'Preliminary checklist of Tudor and Stuart entertainments: 1485–1558.' *Research Opportunities in Renaissance Drama*, XXV, 31–114

Madden, F 1842: 'Political poems of the reigns of Henry VI and Edward IV.' *Archaeologia*, XXIX, 318–47

Manzalaoui, MA (ed.) 1977: *Secretum Secretorum. Nine English Versions*

Mayor, JEB (ed.) 1876: *The English Works of John Fisher*

Meagher, JC 1968: 'The First Progress of Henry VII.' *Renaissance Drama*, new series, I, 45–73

Millican, CB 1932: *Spenser and the Table Round*, Cambridge Mass.

Murray, RH 1936: *The King's Crowning*

Myers, AR 1959: *The Household of Edward IV. The Black Book and the Ordinance of 1478*, Manchester

Nichols, J 1780: *A Collection of the Wills of the Kings and Queens of England from William the Conqueror to Henry VII*

Nichols, J 1788: *The Progresses and Public Processions of Queen Elizabeth*, 1st edn

Nichols, JG (ed.) 1846: *Chronicle of Calais*

Nichols, JG (ed.) 1857: *The Literary Remains of Edward VI*

Nowell, A 1853: *Catechism*, ed. GE Corrie, Cambridge

Orrell, J 1988: *The Human Stage. English Theatre Design, 1567–1640*, Cambridge

Owst, GR 1961: *Literature and Pulpit in Medieval England*, 2nd revised edn, Cambridge

Pauli, R 1878: *Drei volkswirthschaftliche Denkschriften aus der Zeit Heinrichs VIII. von England*, Göttingen

Pecock, R 1860: *The Repressor of over much Blaming of the Clergy*, ed. C Babington

Peele, G 1888: *Works*, ed. AH Bullen

Petowe, H 1603: *Elizabetha quasi vivens. Eliza's Funerall*, repr. in Hazlitt 1875

Pickthorn, K 1934: *Early Tudor Government*, Cambridge

Planché JR 1838: *Regal Records: or a Chronicle of the Coronations of the Queens Regnant of England*

Ramsay, JH 1892: *Lancaster and York*, Oxford

Rastell, J 1811: *The Pastyme of People*, ed. TF Dibdin

Roaf, M 1989: 'The Art of the Achaemenians.' In: *The Arts of Persia*, ed. RW Ferrier

Robinson, WRB 1972: 'Dr Thomas Phaer's Report on the Harbours and Customs Administration of Wales under Edward VI.' *The Bulletin of the Board of Celtic Studies*, XXIV, 485–503

Ross, C 1981: *Richard III*

Royal Commission 1830–52: *State Papers: King Henry VIII*, published under the authority of the Royal Commission

Russell, JC 1969: *The Field of Cloth of Gold*

Saffroy, G 1968–79: *Bibliographie généalogique, héraldique et nobiliaire de la France*

Sander, N 1567: *A Treatise of the Images of Christ and his Saints: and that it is unlawfull to brake them, and lawfull to honour them*, Louvain

Sander, N 1877: *Rise and Growth of the Anglican Schism*, trs. D Lewis

Sanford, F 1677: *A Genealogical History of the Kings of England*

Schramm, PE 1937: *A History of the English Coronation*, Oxford

Scot, R 1584: *The Discoverie of Witchcraft*, ed. RB Nicholson 1886, repr. Wakefield 1973

Skelton, J 1948: *The Complete Poems*, ed. P Henderson

Spenser, E 1579: *Shepheards Calender*

Stanley, AP 1882: *Historical Memorials of Westminster Abbey*, 5th edn

Starkey, D 1982: 'Ightham Mote: politics and architecture in early Tudor England.' *Archaeologia*, CVII, 153–63

Statutes of the Realm 1810–28, eds. A Luders *et al.*

Stevens, J 1961: *Music and Poetry in the Early Tudor Court*

Stow, J 1592: *The Annales of England*

Strong, RC 1963: *Portraits of Queen Elizabeth I*, Oxford

Strong, RC 1977: *The Cult of Elizabeth. Elizabethan Portraiture and Pageantry*

Strong, RC 1984: *Art and Power. Renaissance Festivals 1450–1650*, Woodbridge

Strype, J 1820–40: *Ecclesiastical Memorials*, Oxford

Tatlock, JSP 1933: 'The dragons of Wessex and Wales.' *Speculum*, VIII, 223–35

Tatlock, JSP 1950: *The Legendary History of Britain. Geoffrey of Monmouth's Historia Regum Britanniae and its early vernacular versions*, Berkeley

Tawney, RH and Power, E 1924: *Tudor Economic Documents*

Temperley, G 1917: *Henry VII*

Thomas, AH and Thornley, ID eds 1938: *The Great Chronicle of London*

Thomas, W 1553: *The Pilgrim: a Dialogue on the Life and Actions of King Henry VIII*, ed. JA Froude, 1861

Thompson, WG 1906: *A History of Tapestry*

Thorndike, L 1923–58: *A History of Magic and Experimental Science*, New York

Tottel, R 1559: *The Queens maiesties passage through the citie of London to westminster the daye before her coronacion*

Tout, TFT 1932–34: 'The captivity and death of Edward of Carnarvon.' *The Collected Papers of Thomas Frederick Tout*, Manchester, 145–90

Trexler, RC 1978: *The 'Libro Cerimoniale' of the Florentine Republic by Francesco Filarete and Angelo Manfidi. Introduction and Text*, Geneva

Valeriano Bolzani, P 1556: *Hieroglyphica sive de sacris Aegyptiorum literis commentarii*, Basle

Vergil, P 1844: *Three Books of Polydore Vergil's English History*, ed. H Ellis

Vergil, P 1950: *The Anglica Historia of Polydore Vergil*, ed. and trs. D Hay

Wagner, AR 1950: *A Catalogue of English Mediaeval Rolls of Arms*

Wagner, AR 1956: *Heralds and Heraldry*, 2nd edn

Wagner, AR 1967: *Heralds of England*

Wagner, AR and Sainty, JC 1967: 'The origin of the introduction of peers in the House of Lords.' *Archaeologia*, CI, 119–50

Wall, JC 1891: *The Tombs of the Kings of England*

Walter of Hemingburgh, 1848: *Chronicon*, ed. HC Hamilton

Warkworth J 1839: *Chronicle of the First Thirteen Years of the Reign of Edward IV*, ed. J.O. Halliwell.

Williams, WL 1903: 'A Welsh insurrection.' *Y Cymmrodor*, XVI, 1–93

Withington, R 1918: *English Pageantry: an Historical Outline*, Cambridge Mass.

Woodman, F 1986: *The Architectural History of King's College Chapel*

Worde, Wde 1533: *The noble tryumphaunt coronacyon of quene Anne wyfe unto the moost noble kynge Henry the viij*

Wright, T 1859: *Political Poems and Songs relating to English History*

Wyon, AB and Wyon, A 1887: *The Great Seals of England from the Earliest Period to the Present Time*

Yates, FA 1947: *The French Academies of the Sixteenth Century*

Yates, FA 1975: *Astraea. The Imperial Theme in the Sixteenth Century*

Young, A 1987: *Tudor and Jacobean Tournaments*

Manuscripts cited in text and notes

Manuscripts at the British Library

Additional 18,268.A   Genealogy of Edward IV

Additional 33,736   Petrus Carmelianus's poem on the birth of Prince Arthur

Additional 35,324   Funerals (pictorial records)

Additional 45,131   Funerals

Additional 46,354   *Wriothesley's Book*, a Tudor heraldic collection

Cottonian Augustus II, i   Design for Henry VI's monument

Egerton 2642   Funerals

Egerton 3320   Coronation procession of Elizabeth I

Harleian 48   Funerals

Harleian 336   Giovanni de' Giglis's poem on the marriage of Henry VII

Kings 396   Genealogy of Elizabeth I

Lansdowne 97   Treatise by Clement Urmeston
Lansdowne 874   Heraldic Collection
Lansdowne Rolls 6   Genealogy of Henry VIII
Royal 1.C.viii   Wycliffite Bible
Royal 11.E.xi   Music by Richard Sampson and Benedict de Opiciis
Royal 12.A.xxx   Verses to Elizabeth I on her visit to Windsor 1563
Royal 12.A.xlvii   Verses to Elizabeth on her visit to Woodstock and
    Oxford 1566
Royal 13.C.viii   Miracles of Henry VI
Royal 15.D.i   Biblical history belonging to Edward IV
Royal 15.D.iv   Quintus Curtius
Royal 15.E.vi fol.3 Genealogy of Henry VI
Royal 17.F.v   Godfrey of Bouillon
Royal 18.A.lxxv   Genealogy of Henry VII
Royal 19.A.xxii   Jean de Meun
Royal 19.B.xvi   *Le mirouer des dames*
Royal 19.C.vi   Xenophon, *Anabasis*
Royal 20.E.i—vi   *Chroniques de France*

University of London Library, Senate House

Bromhead Collection, Manuscript Roll of the Funeral of Anne of
    Cleves

Manuscripts at the College of Arms

M.6   Tudor heraldic collection
1st M.13   Tudor ceremonial, including the reception and marriage of
    Katharine of Aragon, and the death and funeral of Prince Arthur

Manuscripts at the Public Record Office

E.36/197   Clement Urmeston's *Sermons and declaracions agaynst popishe
    ceremonyes*
LC.2/1   Funeral collections

London Corporation Record Office

Repertories of the Court of Common Council, Volume IV

INDEX